GRIEF RECOVERY *for* ADULTS

Mastering the Art of Healing and Renewal After Loss with Compassionate Strategies for Emotional Wellness and Finding a Renewed Sense of Purpose

JAMES LAVECK

LaVeck Media, LLC

Text and Design: James LaVeck (www.jameslaveck.com)
Interior images were generated via AI.

ISBN-13:   978-1-7357707-6-5 (Paperback)
              978-1-7357707-7-2 (eBook)
              978-1-7357707-8-9 (Hardcover)

Dedications

It's been over three years since the release of my memoir, Life After Losses. Three incredible years full of love and support from friends and family and three years of working on a project that took a lifeline to learn.

In those three years, and at the time of this publication, I've written over 170 blog entries, over 125,000 words, and countless social media entries. I've sold hundreds of books and reached thousands of readers, all because I had a feeling my story might help someone else's suffering.

And so, with this, I offer my third book, which is dedicated to you, dear reader. May you find strength in your journey, and may you find peace within.

Table of Contents

Introduction

"You will lose someone you can't live without, and your heart will be badly broken, and the bad news is that you never completely get over the loss of your beloved. But this is also the good news. They live forever in your broken heart that doesn't seal back up. And you come through. It's like having a broken leg that never heals perfectly – that still hurts when the weather gets cold, but you learn to dance with the limp." ~ Anne Lamott

I couldn't tell you how many mornings I found myself sitting on the edge of my bed, the weight of loss so heavy on my shoulders that it felt like I could hardly breathe while the world outside was bustling and waking up. Inside, however, everything had come to a standstill. The world kept moving, though mine had ended. I was learning to understand grief not just as an emotion but as a journey—a path that could lead to transformation and renewed purpose if only I dared to walk it. Finally, I found my "ENOUGH!" moment.

My name is James LaVeck, and if you're holding this book, chances are you know this heartache all too well. You might be wondering how someone like me, just an average guy, could guide you through the maelstrom of loss. Well, I've walked this path more times than I cared to, having been widowed twice. I've felt the ground give way beneath me and learned to find my footing again. Along the way, I wrote of my loves, losses, and healing in *Life After Losses: A Memoir of Self-Healing* and *Moving Past Grief: A Collection of Stories and Strategies to Help You Heal.* Beyond writing those books, I've been sharing my personal narrative as a life coach and blogger, feeling privileged to do so.

This book is built on the PURPOSE framework—something I created and stumbled upon while trying to find meaning in sorrow and life. It stands for

- Perceive Reality
- Unload Your Emotional Baggage
- Reach out for Support
- Probe for Personal Significance
- Open a New Chapter
- Save Cherished Memories
- Embrace Personal Growth

Through it, I wish to share a method and a journey toward healing that acknowledges the depth of your pain and the potential for your growth.

To you, dear reader, who may be mourning the loss of a loved one, dealing with the echoes of a divorce, or navigating through any significant life alteration, I see you. This book is for you — created with the understanding that while grief is a road we walk together, each step, each breath, and each tear is profoundly personal. But it also needn't be in solitude.

My objective here is simple: to help guide you through your grief, offering a compassionate hand and strategies for emotional wellness and helping you uncover a renewed sense of purpose. Some of these worked for me, and others I discovered while working on this book. This isn't just about "moving on"; it's about moving *forward* with intention, transforming your grief into a catalyst for personal discovery and growth.

So, I invite you to approach these pages with an open heart and a willing spirit, ready to engage with the exercises, reflections, and strategies before you. Some of them may feel overwhelming to where you are in your journey, and that's okay because the PURPOSE framework will allow you to experience your journey with no pre-set expectations. I want this to be more than a book; it should be a companion on your journey toward healing and transformation to your renewed sense of purpose.

The PURPOSE framework helps when you look at each pillar, and journaling, or at least answering prompts regularly, is pivotal in moving forward. We'll talk about those prompts and journaling later.

There's no right or wrong way, but if you want to work in a pre-designed journal with the prompts, you might consider purchasing the companion, *The PURPOSE Journal*.

As we begin this journey together, I offer a message of hope: Despite the shadow of loss, there is a path forward—a path that leads to a life rich with meaning, purpose, and joy. You are not alone, and with each step, I want to try to help you find your way through the darkness toward the light of a new day.

I'm sorry to welcome you on this journey because I know you had to give up something special to be here.

Chapter 1
Now That's What I Call Grieving

"We get no choice. If we love, we grieve." ~ Thomas Lynch

Before embarking on any journey, I find it helpful to lay out a map to get a lay of the land. Before GPS on our phones, this was how we navigated our journey. Depending on various conditions, my path may alter from a direct route. Think of this chapter as that overview of the land of grief. There is no direct route from grief to healing but a series of paths and alterations in response to our individual needs. This chapter aims to shed light on the individual diversity and complex landscape of grief, navigating through its many forms and the myriad ways it manifests in our lives.

What Is Grief?

A t its core, grief is a response to loss, but not just any loss. It's the deep emotional turmoil that follows the loss of something or someone we hold dear. Whether it's the death of a loved one, the end of a cherished relationship, or the loss of a vital part of our identity, grief is the heart's outcry in the face of absence. Throughout most of the text that follows, the focus is on the loss of a loved one. If you're experiencing a different kind of loss, we'll need to adapt changes to fit your situation.

Defining Loss

Considering loss, it's crucial to understand its broad spectrum. Loss can be tangible, such as the death of a family member, or intangible, like the loss of a dream or an aspect of one's self-identity after a significant life change. Both forms of loss are valid and can cause us to feel grief, underscoring the importance of recognizing and validating the vast array of experiences that constitute loss.

Varieties of Grief

Grief wears many faces, each with its nuances. As we're grieving, there can be expectations put upon us, either by others or, even worse, ourselves. It helps to understand the various types of grief because, as we've noted, grieving is individual.

- **Normal** or **common grief** encapsulates the typical mourning process. It is characterized by waves of sadness, longing, and, eventually, acceptance.

- **Anticipatory grief** occurs before the loss, often seen in the context of terminal illness, where the grief process begins in the shadow of impending loss.
- **Complicated grief**, or **prolonged grief disorder**, describes a scenario where the intensity of grief does not diminish over time, leading to significant impairment.
- **Chronic grief** persists over a long period.
- **Absent grief** refers to a lack of expected mourning reactions (more about expectations to follow).
- **Delayed grief** is when reactions are postponed.
- **Distorted grief** is marked by exaggerated responses or self-destructive behavior.
- **Collective grief** is shared among a group.
- **Disenfranchised grief** is not recognized or validated by society.
- **Exaggerated grief** is an intensified reaction.
- **Silent** or **masked grief** is not openly acknowledged or recognized.
- **Cumulative grief** accumulates over time from multiple losses.
- **Abbreviated grief** is brief and quickly resolved.

You may feel any of these or even a combination of them. There's no one way to grieve, and the only measurement I use personally is whether I am "moving forward" in a healthy manner. "Moving forward" to me means I'm focused on the present. Your definition may vary. A few of these types of grief may raise flags for you, and if you feel you're not "moving forward," as you define it, I would suggest seeking professional help. But, more on that later.

Recognizing the Signs

The symptoms of grief extend beyond mere sadness. Grief affects both the physical and emotional realms. Physically, grief can manifest as exhaustion, changes in appetite, sleep disturbances, or a nebulous ache. Emotionally, it ranges from profound sadness to guilt, anger, numbness, or even relief. These reactions are as varied as the individuals experiencing them, emphasizing the deeply personal nature of grief, and we'll get into those further as we go along.

Grief Versus Depression

While grief and depression share many of the same features, such as intense sadness and withdrawal from usual activities, they are distinctly different experiences. Grief is typically tied to a specific loss and includes many emotions, including moments of joy and remembrance. Depression, however, is pervasive, affecting all aspects of an individual's life, often without a clear trigger. The critical difference lies in how we feel about ourselves; we tend to maintain our self-esteem in grief. In depression, feelings of worthlessness and self-loathing are common. Recognizing when grief transitions into depression is crucial, as it may require seeking professional help to navigate the path toward healing. When I lost my second husband, I knew I needed help and was diagnosed with "situational depression." My entire life was upended, and I really struggled to figure out who I was now as a single parent, and whether I could do it.

Styles of Grieving

With the varieties of grief and our individuality, we shouldn't expect there to be only one grieving style. There's not, which adds to the complexity, negating a one-stop shop for grief recovery:

- The **intuitive griever** processes loss through their experiences, feeling the emotional weight of the loss deeply.
- **Instrumental grievers**, on the other hand, may focus on the cognitive and problem-solving aspects of grief, perhaps channeling their emotions into activities or projects.
- **Dissonant grievers** find themselves caught between how they feel and how they believe they should react, leading to internal conflict.
- Lastly, **blended grievers** exhibit characteristics of both intuitive and instrumental styles, navigating their grief with a mix of emotional expression and action-oriented coping. I found myself to be a blended griever.

As we learn more about grief and all its variations, we understand that grief is not a sign of weakness but a testament to the depth of our connections. Poet Thomas Lynch nailed it: *"If we love, we grieve."*

The Spectrum of Grief: Recognizing Your Unique Pain

I n life, the only constant is change. In the realm of grief, the only constant is variation. Each of us, armed with our unique emotional palette, paints a different picture of loss. This spectrum of grief defies the notion of a one-size-fits-all approach to healing. Understanding and respecting this diversity is the first step toward genuine self-compassion and healing.

Individual Experience

Grief is as individual as a fingerprint—unique patterns etched by personal experiences, relationships, and emotional landscapes. Some find solace in solitude, while others seek comfort in community. Some weep openly, while others suffer in silence, known only to the night. No two griefs are the same, and therein lies a profound truth: comparing one's grief to another's is a journey down a path with no destination.

Resisting the urge to compare allows each person's grief to unfold in its own time and space, free from the constraints of expectation. When I wrote *Life After Losses*, this was one of the cornerstones of the advice I shared. My journey included not dating for two years, which differed from my friend's, who remarried within six months. Neither journey affected the other, and I knew comparing the two was futile. We'll go into this deeper in a moment.

Validation of Pain

Validating your grief, regardless of its outward expressions or societal perceptions, is crucial to healing. Grief, in any form, deserves recognition. It demands to be felt, to be seen, to be acknowledged. This validation is not about seeking approval from others but rather granting oneself permission to grieve wholly and authentically. It's about saying, "My grief is real. My pain is valid. And it's okay not to be okay." This self-validation becomes a cornerstone of emotional wellness, a sanctuary where healing begins. Accept the pain is there, without judgment. I see your grief and acknowledge it. Do you?

Cultural Influences

Culturally, there are bound to be differences in how we grieve and, again, no judgment. I've found beautiful ways to mourn from other cultures and have taken to using "May their memory be a blessing" when addressing someone's loss. In some cultures, grief is like a tumultuous whitewater river on display for all to see. Mourning rituals and communal gatherings provide a shared space for expressing sorrow and remembrance. In others, grief is a silent stream, running deep beneath a stoic exterior, where private remembrance takes precedence over public displays. Understanding these cultural nuances helps shape the grieving process and influences how individuals navigate their loss. Acknowledging and respecting these cultural differences enriches the collective understanding of grief, fostering a more inclusive and empathetic approach to healing.

Support Systems

As we've seen, the combination of grief types, individuality, culture, experience, etc., can create some chaos in finding a healing path. Navigating that storm is not something I believe one should face or try alone. Personalized support systems, based on your needs and preferences, can be a lifeline in the sea of loss. These support systems can take many forms, from close-knit family units and friends to support groups and professional counseling. What's crucial is to align the support with your individual needs, ensuring a safe space for expressing grief and exploring healing.

For some, a support group provides a sense of community and shared understanding. In this place, the language of loss is spoken fluently. This is where I found myself with my first loss. For others, one-on-one counseling offers a more intimate setting for unpacking the layers of grief, guided by a professional who can navigate the complex emotional landscapes. This is where I found myself the second time. Then, some find comfort in the silent companionship of a pet or solace in the pages of a journal.

The beauty of these support systems lies in their diversity, as each of us is diverse. Each reflects the uniqueness of the grieving process. They underscore the fact that while grief may be a road we walk alone, support systems help light the way, offering moments of respite and companionship along the journey. We don't need to follow the same path, but taking inspiration from others can be immensely helpful.

It's crucial to remember that your pain is yours alone. It doesn't need to mirror anyone else's to be valid. It doesn't need to conform to cultural norms to be respected. And it certainly doesn't need to walk alone to be acknowledged. Your unique pain is seen in the vast spectrum of grief; it is valid and worthy of support and compassion. In the coming chapters, we'll share some strategies for finding the right support systems for you.

The Physicality of Grief: Listening to Your Body's Mourning

Grief doesn't just reside in the echoes of an empty room or the quiet moments before sleep envelops you. It seeps into your very being, manifesting in your physical body. Your body reflects the weight of grief and the turmoil it is. Another piece of advice I've shared over the years is to be kind to yourself and take care of your needs. That also includes your physical needs and eating right, for example. There's a reason for that, as you'll read below.

Your Body's Response

Why does grief take such a tangible toll on our bodies? The answer lies in the connection between our emotional and physical health. Grief is a stress of the highest order, and stress, in turn, triggers physiological responses designed to protect us. In the short term, these reactions are survival mechanisms, but when the stress is prolonged, as with grief, they can become harmful. In its attempt to cope with the loss, your body might signal distress through fatigue, forcing you to slow down and process. Or it might alter your appetite, as eating patterns are closely tied to emotional states. Recognizing these signals as part of your body's response to grief is the first step in addressing them.

Physical Symptoms

There are many physical symptoms of grief, but even with the individual variations, some common experiences include:

- **Fatigue**: A pervasive tiredness that rest doesn't seem to alleviate, reflecting the exhaustive work of mourning.
- **Changes in Appetite**: Whether it's a loss of appetite or seeking comfort in food, changes in eating habits are a direct response to emotional distress.
- **Sleep Disturbances**: Difficulty falling asleep, staying asleep, or experiencing nightmares as the mind struggles to process the loss.
- **Aches and Pains**: Unexplained physical pains, often the body's way of expressing emotional pain.
- **Weakened Immune System**: Increased susceptibility to illnesses, as chronic stress impacts the body's ability to fight infections.

Recognizing these symptoms in yourself acknowledges grief's impact on your entire being.

Self-Care Practices

Navigating the physical aspects of grief requires a more gentle, nurturing approach to self-care. Here are some practices that can help ease the physical symptoms:

- **Rest**: Listen to your body's need for rest, even if sleep is elusive. Short naps or simply lying down in a peaceful environment can help.
- **Nutrition**: Try to keep yourself to a balanced diet, even when your appetite fluctuates. Small, nutrient-rich meals can be more manageable and help stabilize energy levels.
- **Movement**: Gentle exercise, like walking or yoga, can release endorphins, improve mood, and help with sleep.
- **Hydration**: Keep hydrated, as dehydration can worsen fatigue and lethargy.

- **Breathing Exercises**: Practice deep, slow breathing to help manage moments of anxiety or panic and anchor you in the present.

Creating a self-care routine doesn't mean adhering to a strict regimen. It's about listening to your body's needs and responding with kindness and patience. Remember: be kind to yourself.

Seeking Professional Help

Sometimes, the physical symptoms of grief persist, growing into concerns that interfere with daily life. If you struggle to manage these symptoms, or if they worsen over time, it may be time to seek professional help. A healthcare provider can assess your symptoms, rule out other conditions, and offer treatment options. This might include therapy to address the emotional roots of your physical symptoms, medication to help with sleep or anxiety, or a referral to a specialist if needed. I remember being unable to sleep, no matter what I did, and I knew I needed some help.

Here's what I knew: I couldn't care for our children if I couldn't care for myself. It's the "put your mask on before helping others" of the pre-flight safety briefing. Seeking help is not an admission of failure but an act of courage. It's an acknowledgment that you're not meant to carry this burden alone and that people are ready and willing to walk alongside you on this path.

Grief reminds us of the link between our emotional and physical well-being. By paying attention to the physical manifestations of grief, we honor our body's role in the mourning process and take an essential step toward healing. Listening to your body, caring for it with kindness, and seeking support when needed are all part of the journey toward recovery.

The Stages of Grief Debunked: A More Flexible Approach

The concept of grief evolving through a series of stages has become deeply ingrained in our cultural understanding of mourning. It's a framework that suggests a linear progression: denial, anger, bargaining, depression, and acceptance. Initially proposed by Elisabeth Kübler-Ross, this model has offered valuable insights. However, it doesn't address grief's complex, and frequently unpredictable, nature. The model was, after all, developed for people who were dying, not those of us left behind. Here, we'll explore why a more nuanced, flexible approach to understanding grief is beneficial and necessary for healing.

Myth of Stages

The stage-based model of grief has been both a comfort and a constraint to those navigating loss. On one hand, it provides a structure to the seemingly chaotic experience of grief. On the other, it implies a rigidity that doesn't align with the reality many of us face. The truth is grief doesn't adhere to a strict sequence. You might feel acceptance one day, only to wake up wrapped up in anger or denial the next. This fluctuation is normal and reflects the deeply personal process of grieving. By challenging the notion that grief must unfold in predetermined stages, we open the door to a more authentic, individualized experience of mourning. Once again, this is another piece of my advice: Grief is not linear.

Personal Journey

Acknowledging that each person's experience with grief is unique is crucial, as I mentioned above. No two grief patterns are exactly alike. Some people might skip stages altogether, while others might experience them in a different order or revisit the same emotions multiple times. It is essential, then, to view grief as a personal journey, defined not by a series of stages but by individual experiences, feelings, and coping mechanisms. Embracing this perspective encourages those in mourning to listen to their own needs and emotions rather than feeling pressured to conform to a specific pattern of grieving or (as we've discussed) comparing your journey with another.

Flexibility in Healing

A flexible approach to grief acknowledges that healing is not a linear process. It champions the idea that moving through grief involves an ebb and flow of emotions like the movements of the ocean. Some days, the waters might be calm, while others bring turbulent waves. This analogy highlights the need for adaptability in coping strategies and support systems. It suggests that what works one day might not work the next, and that's okay. Flexibility in healing means allowing yourself to find what works for you at the moment, whether seeking solitude, engaging in creative expression, or leaning on friends and family for support.

New Models

In recent years, new models of understanding grief have emerged, challenging the traditional stage-based approach. These models emphasize grief's fluid and cyclical nature, recognizing that it's a process that can loop back on itself, revisiting emotions and experiences in different contexts over time. One such model is the Dual Process Model, proposed by Margaret Stroebe and Henk Schut. It suggests that bereaved individuals oscillate between confronting and avoiding their grief. This model acknowledges the dynamic nature of coping with loss, allowing for moments of respite alongside active mourning.

Another perspective, the Continuing Bonds theory, shifts the focus from detachment from the deceased to the ongoing relationship that survivors maintain with their loved ones. This approach highlights the importance of integrating the memory of the deceased into one's life as a way of adapting to loss. It celebrates the idea that healing doesn't mean letting go of the person who has passed but instead finding a new way to hold them in your heart.

These models, among others, offer fresh lenses through which to view grief, unlike what I found in the books I read in the mid-1990s. They provide a vocabulary that speaks to the multifaceted, evolving nature of mourning, emphasizing that healing is not a destination but a journey marked by growth, change, and adaptation. *This* reflected my experience better than the five-stage model.

Moving away from the rigid framework of stages allows for a more compassionate, nuanced understanding of grief. This shift doesn't invalidate the stage-based model. Instead, it builds upon it with additional perspectives that resonate with the diverse experiences of those in mourning. By embracing a flexible approach to the grieving process, we honor the complexity of the human heart and its capacity to heal in the face of loss.

The Myth of the Grief Timeline: Why It's Okay Not to Be Okay

S ociety has a way of wrapping grief in a timeline, a neatly packaged journey with a beginning, middle, and end. But here's the thing: grief doesn't clock in and out on schedule. It doesn't care for the neatly drawn lines or the checkpoints we're told to pass. It doesn't care how many stages it's supposed to take. It's another way of comparing your journey that makes no sense to your individuality. This section is about breaking down these timelines and giving you the space to feel your grief fully and unapologetically on your terms.

Rejecting Timelines

The notion that grief operates on a predictable timeline does more harm than good. You might have heard phrases like, "It's been a year, aren't you over it yet?" or "Time heals all wounds." Though often well-intentioned, these sayings can feel like chains, binding you to an unrealistic expectation of healing. In reality, grief has its rhythm, a beat that varies from person to person. For some, the acute pain of loss fades into a dull ache in months. For others, it's a presence felt daily, years down the line. By rejecting the idea of a timeline, we open ourselves up to a more authentic grieving process, one that acknowledges the true nature of our pain and healing.

Permission to Grieve

Right here, right now, let's set something straight: you have permission to grieve in a way that feels right to you. If that means crying in the middle of a grocery store aisle because a song reminded you of them, that's okay. I remember crying in the middle of the beer aisle at Trader Joe's. If it means laughing at a memory when you're expected to be solemn, that's okay, too. Grief is a multifaceted experience marked by moments of sadness, joy, regret, and even relief. The societal pressure to grieve in a certain way, to put on a brave face, or to move on after a designated period only serves to isolate us in our pain, and I call B.S. on it. Let's break those chains. Let's give ourselves and each other the permission to experience grief in all its complexity, free from judgment (including our own!).

The Healing Process

We've talked about this a little bit: healing from grief is not a linear path; it's more like a spiral, looping back on itself, revisiting emotions and memories with each turn. In fact, it looks a lot like the results you'd get from the Spirograph toy I played with when I was a kid. You might feel like you've made progress, only to be hit with a wave of sadness on an anniversary or holiday. This is normal. Each time you revisit these emotions, you're not regressing; you're healing. With each loop, you can understand your grief from a new perspective and more meaningfully integrate your loss into your life. This process is not about reaching a destination where grief no longer exists (hint: no such place exists). It's about learning to carry your grief with you, allowing it to shape you without defining you, which is what my work has been about.

Long-term Impact

Grief can change you meaningfully, changing how you see the world, your relationships, and yourself. Its long-term nature means it can evolve, manifesting itself in different ways as you move through the stages of your life. For instance, a young widow navigating grief might focus on the immediate challenges of loss. At the same time, years later, the same person might reflect on how their grief has shaped their identity and relationships. Similarly, parents who have lost a child might find that their grief shifts as they navigate life's milestones without their child. This evolution doesn't mean you're leaving your loved one behind; instead, it's a testament to the depth of your love, which continues to grow and change with you.

I was 28 the first time I was widowed, 47 the second. I was 54 when I released *Life After Losses.* At 54, I had the life experience to see how my losses shaped who I was; at 28, I didn't know how to survive the loss.

Grief is unpredictable and defies expectations; it is also a testament to our capacity for love. It reminds us that the people we lose never really leave us; they become a part of us, shaping our hearts and our journeys in ways we might not understand for years to come. So, let's give ourselves the grace to grieve in our own time, reject the timelines, and embrace the beautifully messy healing process.

The Grief Competition: Why Your Loss Is Not Comparable

In the realm of grief, it's tempting to measure our pain against that of others, place our sorrow on a scale, and see where it falls. However, this is where we must stop and remind ourselves of the truth: grief is not a competition. The intensity of your pain doesn't need validation through comparison. Each loss carries its unique shadow, and every heartbreak has its own depth. Recognizing this is crucial. Healing isn't a race but a path we navigate with respect for our own pace and that of others.

Avoiding Comparisons

It's a natural inclination to look around and wonder why others seem to be "handling things better" or to feel that our loss must be the greatest to warrant the depths of our despair. I fell into that trap when Bea, an elderly woman with kind, expressive eyes, told me, "It gets better," at my first support group meeting. "Clearly, she didn't love her husband as much as I did mine," I thought. It was a mistake, obviously. This comparison mindset only isolates us further, building walls where we need bridges. Remember, the outward expressions of grief are just the surface; beneath, the waters run as deep and turbulent as yours. When we catch ourselves slipping into the trap of comparison, we must step back and remind ourselves that grief is as diverse as the individuals who experience it. Acknowledging that each person's pain is valid allows for a kinder inner dialogue that fosters healing.

Compassion for All

Extending compassion is a centerpiece of navigating grief, not just toward ourselves, which is paramount, but also toward others. It's about understanding that behind every grieving face is a world of pain as complex and nuanced as our own, the depths of which we cannot know. This compassion means holding space for all forms of grief without judgment or ranking. Whether it's the loss of a pet, a job, a relationship, or a loved one, each form of loss deserves acknowledgment and empathy. A loss is a loss for the person feeling it. Encouraging a compassionate environment results in open, honest expressions of pain and supports a collective healing process where no one feels marginalized.

Healing Together

There's strength in shared vulnerability, in the collective acknowledgment of our wounds. When we stop comparing our grief, we open the door to truly connecting with others. Healing becomes a collective endeavor, a journey we navigate with the support of those who understand the terrain of loss. This doesn't mean that we all heal in the same way or at the same speed; instead, we recognize the value in each other's experiences. We learn from each other. It's about finding common ground in the universal experience of loss and using it as a foundation for building a supportive community.

By moving away from the inclination to compare our grief to that of others, we allow ourselves the freedom to grieve authentically. We give ourselves the space to feel our pain fully and to navigate the complexities of loss without the added weight of judgment. This shift toward compassion and understanding for ourselves and others paves the way for an inclusive, respectful, and profoundly human healing process. It reminds us that in the vast landscape of human emotion, grief is but one facet, a shared experience that binds us in our vulnerability and capacity for love.

Grief Waves: Navigating the Highs and Lows

I magine standing at the shore, watching as waves crash against the sand. Some waves gently lap at your feet, while others surge with unexpected force, momentarily overwhelming you. This ebb and flow, this unpredictable rhythm, mirrors the experience of grief. It's not a steady state but a series of waves, varying in intensity and impact, each carrying its unique blend of emotions. There will be days when the sea is calm, and grief feels like a distant memory, only for a rogue wave to catch you off guard, reminding you of the depth of your loss. This fluid nature of grief underscores the importance of flexibility and self-compassion in healing.

Coping with Intensity

When a particularly intense wave of grief hits, it can feel as though you're being swept away. Here are a few strategies to help you navigate these moments:

- **Ground Yourself**: Find a physical anchor in your environment, something you can see, touch, taste, or smell. This can help bring you back to the present moment when emotions run high.
- **Deep Breathing**: Focus on your breath, taking slow, deep breaths. This simple act can help calm your nervous system and provide a sense of control amidst the chaos of intense emotions.
- **Reach Out**: If a wave catches you off guard, don't hesitate to reach out to a friend, family member, or support group. Sometimes, just sharing your feelings can help diminish their intensity.

- **Allow the Wave to Pass**: Remind yourself that grief waves will pass like the ocean's waves. Allow yourself to feel the emotions without judgment, knowing they will ebb in time.

Finding Stability

Amidst the unpredictability of grief waves, finding emotional stability can seem like a daunting task. Yet, there are ways to create a sense of balance:

- **Routine**: Establishing a daily routine can offer a sense of normalcy and structure. Simple tasks, such as making your bed or preparing a meal, can provide comfort and a sense of accomplishment.
- **Self-Care**: Prioritizing self-care is crucial. This might mean different things to different people—whether it's a walk in nature, a warm bath, or engaging in a hobby that brings joy.
- **Mindfulness and Meditation**: Practices like mindfulness and meditation can help anchor you in the present, reducing the overwhelming feelings that can accompany intense grief waves.
- **Journaling**: Writing about your feelings can offer a way to process them, providing both a release and a way to track your healing process over time. We'll talk about that in a few moments.

Embracing Emotions

One of the most challenging aspects of navigating grief waves is learning to embrace the emotions they bring without judgment. It's natural to want to push away feelings of sadness, anger, or despair, but doing so can prolong the healing process. Embracing your emotions means acknowledging them, naming them, and allowing them to be felt fully. It's about understanding that grief is not something to be "fixed" but experienced. This acceptance can be liberating, opening up a space for healing and, eventually, peace. Not embracing or feeling emotions, however, can lead to serious physical issues.

In the journey through grief, it's essential to remember that waves—no matter how powerful—do not define the ocean. They are simply moments in time, each passing to make way for the next. Similarly, grief, with its highs and lows, is a part of the broader experience of love and loss. By learning to ride these waves, we honor our loved ones and ourselves, moving toward a place of acceptance and renewed strength.

Start a PURPOSE Journal

The act of journaling, particularly through the lens of grief, is more than just putting pen to paper; it becomes a sanctuary for your thoughts, a space where emotions can be untangled, and a mirror reflecting your inner world during times of loss. The benefits of keeping a grief journal are manifold, offering a cathartic release and insights into the complexities of your mourning process. My first journal became the basis of *Life After Losses* and has allowed me to gain valuable insight into my life journey.

Now, some of you may balk at the mere suggestion of journaling. Maybe you tried it before, and it didn't stick (guilty), or perhaps you don't want someone to find it. Whatever your objection, I'd like to share some of the benefits of journaling (hint: more than one of these are possible):

- **Catharsis**: Writing about your loss helps in releasing the pent-up emotions that can be too difficult to vocalize. It's a form of emotional exhale, a way to breathe out the pain held too tightly inside.
- **Clarity**: Journaling brings clarity to the whirlwind of thoughts and feelings that come with grief. It helps distinguish between the overlapping threads of sadness, anger, guilt, or confusion, offering a clearer view of your emotional landscape.
- **Memory Preservation**: For many, a grief journal becomes a place to preserve memories of the person or thing lost. It can hold stories, reflections, and moments of remembrance, keeping the essence of what was cherished alive.

- **Healing Tracker**: Your journal can be a tangible tracker of your healing process. It's a place to look back and realize how far you've come, to see the subtle shifts in your coping mechanisms, and to recognize the strength you've gathered along the way.
- **Self-Discovery**: The journey through grief often leads to profound self-discovery. Your journal can become a tool for uncovering aspects of yourself that were previously unknown, revealing how loss has shaped you and where it's leading you next.

Starting Your Journal

I get it: starting to journal while you're an emotional wreck mired in the chaos of grief might seem daunting, especially if you've not journaled before. But it's simpler than you might think (really it is). Here are some steps to gently introduce you to journaling:

- **Choose Your Medium**: Whether it's a classic notebook, a digital app, or an audio diary, select a medium that feels most comfortable and accessible for you. I found the act of pen to paper was cathartic as I saw a physical release of thought to paper.
- **Set aside Time**: Dedicate a specific time of day for journaling. It doesn't have to be lengthy; even a few minutes can be meaningful. The key is consistency, allowing this practice to become a part of your daily routine.
- **Write Unfiltered**: Your journal is a judgment-free zone. Let your thoughts and feelings flow unfiltered, without concern for grammar, coherence, or structure. This is

about expression, not perfection. I'm going to repeat it many times: do not judge.

- **Use Prompts**: I suggest using specific prompts daily within the PURPOSE framework. These will help you focus on the various aspects of your grief recovery, and we'll talk about each element of PURPOSE in the following chapters. Still, these should be able to get you started. Some days, you'll feel more inclined to focus on specific sections, which is perfectly acceptable. Remember: no judgment.

  - **Perceive Reality:** Today, what was one moment where you felt the presence of your loss the most? What triggered it, and how did it make you feel? Additional thought: How has your perception of your current reality shifted today, if at all? Do you find yourself accepting it more, or are you struggling with denial or anger?
  - **Unload Your Emotional Baggage:** What feelings are you struggling with the most right now? Allow yourself to express them here without judgment.
  - **Reach Out for Support:** Who did you connect with today, or who can you contact tomorrow for support? What kind of support do you need the most right now (listening ear, distraction, advice)? Additionally, reflect on any help you may have provided others.
  - **Probe for Personal Significance:** What did your loss teach you about what truly matters in life? Are there insights you gained today about your

values or priorities? Where have you found gratitude, or have you?

- **Open a New Chapter:** What small step can you take tomorrow to move forward or do something different? This could be as simple as taking a new route on your walk, trying out a new hobby, doing a self-care ritual, or setting a small, achievable goal.
- **Save Cherished Memories:** What is a happy memory you have of the person, place, or situation you've lost? How did this memory make you feel today, and what does it remind you of about the relationship or connection? How have you kept the memory alive?
- **Embrace Personal Growth:** In what ways did you notice yourself growing or changing today, even in the slightest sense? This can be related to resilience, understanding, compassion, or any other area.

Maintaining Your Journaling Practice

Keeping up with journaling requires patience and flexibility, especially through the ebbs and flows of grief. Here are some suggestions to sustain your practice:

- **Be Kind to Yourself**: There will be days when journaling feels too heavy, and that's okay. Your journal is there for you without demands or expectations.
- **Mix It Up**: If writing feels monotonous, incorporate other elements. You might add photos, sketches, or even pieces of fabric that hold special memories. Your journal can be as unique as your journey.

- **Reflect**: Periodically, take time to read back through your entries. This reflection can offer new insights into your healing process and a deeper understanding of how grief is evolving within you.
- **Privacy is Key**: Ensure your journal is kept in a place where you feel it's private and secure. Knowing your thoughts are safe allows for more open and honest expression.

Journaling through grief is like conversing with yourself, which honors where you've been, acknowledges where you are, and gently nudges you toward where you might go. It's a practice that does not rush healing but offers a quiet space for mourning, reflection, and, eventually, growth. Through the simple act of writing, you give your grief a voice, allowing it to be heard, felt, and understood in all its complexity.

My journal became a personal record of resilience and change. It was a companion in my moments of solitude, a witness to my tears, and a testament to the love that endures beyond loss. As you navigate through the stormy waters of grief, let your journal stand as a lighthouse, guiding you back to yourself time and time again.

Let's set sail.

Chapter 2: *P*erceive Reality

"You can't truly heal from a loss until you allow yourself to really feel the loss." ~ Mandy Hale, *The Single Woman: Life, Love, and a Dash of Sass*

Imagine standing on the shore of a vast ocean, its waves crashing with relentless force. Now, picture yourself stepping into the water, feeling the cold rush against your skin, the tide's pull urging you to step back. This is what facing the reality of a significant loss can feel like—an overwhelming force we're instinctively wired to resist at first. In this initial step back, denial finds its roots. In the context of grief, denial isn't just a refusal to accept facts; it's a complex emotional and psychological response that serves as our mind's first line of defense against a reality too painful to process immediately. But to heal, we must face that reality. We have to see the world for what it is. Denial is not a river in Egypt.

Why Acceptance Is Hard

The psychology behind the difficulty in accepting the death of a loved one or any significant loss is rooted in our basic human instincts. Biologically, our brains are wired to protect us from pain, and the shock of loss activates this primal defense mechanism. This isn't about intelligence or emotional strength; it's about our most fundamental survival instincts kicking in. The reality of losing someone can challenge our sense of security, our plans for the future, and even our understanding of the world. It's a gigantic earthquake to the mental and emotional landscapes we've built, and acceptance means acknowledging that everything has changed. That's a tall order for anyone. They can't really be gone if their shoes are still by the front door, right?

Denial as a Coping Mechanism

Denial serves as a psychological buffer, a kind of emotional breathing space. It allows us to process the loss in smaller, more manageable pieces. Think of it like slowly dipping your toes into the water, getting used to its temperature bit by bit, rather than diving in all at once. In the short term, denial can help us maintain our daily functions, keeping us from being completely overwhelmed by grief. It's the mind's way of saying, "Let's take this one step at a time."

On the one hand, this can be a good thing. There's always the other hand, though. This is the double-edged sword of denial: it's nature's way of protecting us, but it's also nature's way of stopping us from healing, trapping us in a cycle where the reality of loss is neither faced nor processed.

Signs of Denial

Recognizing the signs of denial can be tricky because it often masquerades as other, more socially acceptable reactions. Here are a few indicators that someone might be experiencing denial in the wake of loss:

- **Avoidance**: Actively avoiding conversations about the deceased, changing the subject, or focusing on trivial matters to steer away from the reality of loss.
- **Rationalization**: Coming up with alternative explanations for the loss or clinging to hope of a mistake in diagnosis (in cases of death) or potential reconciliation (in cases of relationship breakdowns).
- **Numbness**: Displaying a lack of emotional response, not because the person isn't grieving, but as a way to shield themselves from the full impact of their sorrow.
- **Planning for the Future**: Making plans that still include the person who has passed away, showing a refusal to accept that the person is gone.

We need to understand these to recognize denial in ourselves and offer support to others who are grieving. It's about creating a space where the pain of loss can be acknowledged at a pace that doesn't force us to dive deeper than we're ready to handle.

Even for its power to protect, denial can only be a temporary shelter and not a fortress. It's a natural part of the grieving process, a phase that most of us will pass through as we begin to confront the reality of our loss. However, staying in denial indefinitely can hinder healing, leaving grief unresolved. The challenge, then, is not to *avoid* denial but to recognize it for what it is: it's one stop, one signpost, on the journey of grief, signaling a path toward eventual acceptance.

The Danger of Suppressing Your Grief

When it feels like you just cannot escape the weight of loss, when it feels like it's sitting on your chest and you can't breathe, it's tempting to shove it into the darkest corners of our minds, hoping that if we ignore it long enough, it might disappear. While that may feel like a relief and a way of protecting yourself, doing so carries risks that stretch far beyond the emotional realm, seeping into our physical well-being and shaping our paths to recovery in ways we might not have thought.

Risks of Suppression

Suppressing grief is like playing with a Jack-in-the-Box; the more you wind the toy up, the more force the spring gathers, ready to jump with unexpected intensity. The emotional risks of this suppression are vast. They range from sudden outbursts of anger to a persistent sense of sadness that clouds every moment. Physically, the constant tension of holding back emotions can manifest as insomnia, a weakened immune response, or even more severe health complications over time. The danger is not just in these immediate symptoms but in how they can build barriers between us and our ability to process loss.

Recognizing Suppression

Identifying when you're suppressing grief is the first step toward addressing it—let's perceive reality, remember? What are some signs that you might be suppressing your grief? They might include:

- **Unexplained Irritability**: Snapping at minor annoyances could be your bottled-up emotions seeking an outlet.

- **Physical Symptoms Without Cause**: Headaches, stomach issues, or muscle tension that seem to have no direct cause might be your body's response to suppressed grief.
- **Avoidance of Reminders**: Steering clear of places, people, or activities linked to your loss might indicate you're not ready to face your grief.
- **Overactivity**: Throwing yourself into work, hobbies, or social engagements without pause could be a strategy to avoid dealing with your loss.

Recognizing these signs is a call to gently begin the process of unpacking your grief, to allow yourself to feel and express the pain you've been holding back. I found myself experiencing most of these to varying degrees of intensity. Overactivity tends to be my go-to.

Healthy Expression

Finding safe, constructive ways to express grief is essential for healing. Here are a few strategies that can help:

- **Therapy**: Speaking with a professional offers an outlet for your emotions and guidance on navigating through them toward healing.
- **Creative Outlets**: Painting, music, or any form of creative expression can be cathartic, providing a non-verbal way to process complex feelings.
- **Physical Activity**: Exercise, especially activities like running or yoga, can help release the pent-up energy that comes with suppressed emotions.

These are just a few outlets that offer a way to express your grief, not as an overwhelming flood, but as a stream that flows, bit by bit, toward a larger sea of acceptance and peace.

Long-term Healing

The journey toward healing from a significant loss is marked by and requires a courageous decision to face it. Acknowledging and expressing grief is not about accelerating the process but allowing it to flow in its own time. It helps ensure the foundations for long-term healing are laid with care and respect for your individual needs. This approach cultivates resilience, teaching us that while grief can change us, it also offers opportunities for growth, deeper connections with others, and a renewed appreciation for the moments of joy that life brings. More on that later as we dig deeper.

As we navigate through loss, remember this: healing is not a race or a destination. It's a process that unfolds day by day, step by step, guided by our willingness to face our grief, feel it, express it, and eventually integrate it into the fabric of our lives. It may feel like two steps forward and one step back for a while; you may find yourself back at Square One, but know this: you left Square One before, and you know how to do it, and you know it can be done.

Facing the Painful Truth

F acing the truth leads to acceptance, often misunderstood as a signal of defeat or an end to mourning; it is neither. It's not about forgetting or moving on (as if that were possible); it's about acknowledging the reality of our loss and allowing it to coexist with our ongoing lives. Acceptance is a dynamic process that doesn't erase pain but integrates it. It invites us to carry forward the love and memories of what we've lost, weaving them into who we are becoming. This acceptance doesn't come all at once but gradually as we learn to live *with*, instead of *for*, our loss, finding ways to honor our loved ones and ourselves in the process.

Charting New Paths to Acceptance

Facing acceptance requires you to be determined while still being kind to yourself. Here are some strategies to ease the transition from denial to acceptance, some of which have multiple benefits:

- **Mindful Awareness**: Practice being present with your feelings and observe them without judgment. This can help you recognize moments of denial and gently guide your focus back to acceptance.
- **Expressive Outlets**: Engage in activities that allow you to express your grief and memories, such as writing, art, or music. These outlets can help externalize your feelings, making the acceptance process more tangible. In *Life After Losses*, I share how I created a series of mixtapes to share my emotional journey with others.
- **Memory Rituals**: Create rituals that honor the memory of your loved one. This could be as simple as lighting a

candle each night or visiting a special place for both of you. These rituals can serve as a bridge between your past together and your future.

- **Support Networks**: Lean on friends, family, or support groups who can hold space for your grief. Sharing your journey with others who understand can be incredibly validating, reminding you that you're not alone in your acceptance process.

A New Perspective on Death

As we struggle to find acceptance, it's crucial to challenge and change our cultural narratives around death. There is a movement around death positivity that looks to open up conversations about death, which would encourage a more open and accepting attitude toward it. It isn't about glorifying or trivializing death but acknowledging it as a natural part of life. By fostering more open discussions, we can demystify death and grieving, in turn reducing the fear and denial that often goes with it. Here are some ways to embrace a death-positive perspective:

- **Educate Yourself**: Learn about different cultural and historical perspectives on death. Understanding how other societies view death can broaden your view and ease the discomfort of discussing it.
- **Talk about Death**: Initiate conversations about death with friends and family. This could involve discussing end-of-life wishes, sharing fears, or simply reflecting on the nature of mortality.
- **Participate in Death-Positive Events**: Look for events like death cafes, where people gather to discuss death in a relaxed, informal setting. These gatherings can be

powerful venues for breaking down taboos and building a more death-accepting community.

When we bring this type of activity into our lives, we can shift our relationship with death from one of fear and denial to one of acceptance and openness. This shift helps in our personal journey through grief. Also, it contributes to a larger cultural transformation, one where death is neither hidden nor feared but acknowledged as an integral part of the human experience. Death is part of life, after all.

Acceptance and denial are like the yin and yang, each playing a role in our journey. By understanding the protective nature of denial and the healing power of acceptance, we can work through the complex landscape of loss with compassion and resilience. Embracing a death-positive perspective allows us to view death as not an end but a natural, meaningful part of life. Through this lens, we can find the courage to face the painful truth of our loss. We allow it to transform and guide us toward growth, understanding, and, ultimately, a renewed sense of connection and understanding of the cycle of life.

Reflecting on Your PURPOSE Journal

When you're working on your PURPOSE Journal, remember your prompts for **Perceive Reality**: Today, what was one moment where you felt the presence of your loss the most? What triggered it, and how did it make you feel? Additional thought: How has your perception of your current reality shifted today, if at all? Do you find yourself accepting it more, or are you struggling with denial or anger?

Reflect upon what you've learned in this chapter and your feelings. Grab a pen and your journal or a piece of paper, and find a comfortable, serene spot where you can be uninterrupted. Take a moment to breathe deeply and center yourself. Prepare your heart and mind for this journey inward. We will spend some time focusing on the loss and facing the reality of its impact on your life.

The Reality

The path to acceptance is paved with stones of reality, each a truth about your loss and its impact on your life. This exercise helps you gently acknowledge these truths, one step at a time.

- **The Fact of Loss**: Write down the facts of your loss. It might not be easy, but articulating this reality is crucial for acceptance. What happened?
- **Changes**: Reflect on the changes this loss has brought into your life. How has your daily life shifted? What do you miss the most?

Seeking the Silver Linings

Even in loss, there can be moments of light, instances of gratitude, or some learning that emerges from the shadows. Finding these can be a powerful way to move toward acceptance, and you should not feel guilty. Remember: no judgment.

- **Gratitude**: Can you think of anything you're grateful for that's come from this experience? Maybe it's the support you've received or a new perspective on life. Sometimes, I find the act of seeking something for which to be grateful leaves me grateful.
- **Growth**: How have you grown from this experience? Consider how you've become stronger, more empathetic, or more resilient, for example.

This exercise is not meant to be completed in one sitting as a one-and-done. These prompts are here to get you to think about the reality of your life; remember, we're in the Perceive Reality section. Grief and acceptance are fluid; they evolve alongside you. Come back to it whenever you need, add to it, reflect on it, and see how your responses might change over time. It reflects your journey and reminds you that, even in the face of loss, you have the strength to acknowledge, accept, and find a way to carry love and memories into your future.

In this exploration, we've walked through the fields of denial, stood at the edge of the shore of acceptance, and looked toward the horizon where healing beckons. As we move forward, let's carry the courage to face our grief, the strength to embrace acceptance, and the hope that guides us into the next chapter of our journey.

Chapter 3: Unload Your Emotional Baggage

"Only time and tears take away grief; that is what they are for." ~ Terry Pratchett, *I Shall Wear Midnight*

icture this: you're in the middle of cooking dinner, and suddenly, without warning, you're sobbing over the sink, not over the onions you're chopping, but a wave of grief that hit you out of the blue. Or maybe you're laughing with friends, feeling almost normal, when a shadow of guilt pulls you under, whispering, "Should I even be enjoying myself?" Grief is that unexpected guest who doesn't care if it's a good time for you. It shows up, makes itself at home, kicks the cat, and doesn't mind making a mess of your emotions. It's raw, it's real, and, yes, it's incredibly messy. And here's the thing: it's supposed to be.

Grief is a Messy Mess of a Mess!

Ugly Truths

Grief isn't pretty. It doesn't come in neat, manageable packages we can schedule at our convenience. It's the midnight tears, the anger that flares at minor inconveniences, the laughter that turns into crying because you remembered. It's forgetting to eat (or eating too much), sleeping all day, or staring at the ceiling all night. It's messy because life is messy, and love is messy. This mess, this chaos of emotions, is a testament to the depth of our connections and the price of love and loss.

Here's a truth that might not be widely advertised but easily recognized by anyone who's experienced it: grief can make you feel like you've lost your mind. You might misplace things, forget appointments, wear your shirt inside out, and only realize it hours later. Or am I projecting?

You might find yourself talking to your loved one as if they're right there beside you or avoiding places filled with memories too painful to face. This disarray, both internal and external, is a normal part of the grieving process. It's your mind and body trying to navigate a world that's shifted on its axis.

It's Okay

Hear this loud and clear: all of this mess, this disarray, this rollercoaster of emotions—it's okay. It's normal. Grieving isn't a process you can control, streamline, or predict. It doesn't adhere to schedules or societal expectations. It simply is. And what you're feeling—the good, the bad, the ugly—is a part of that process. It's unlikely you've actually lost your mind.

There will be good days and bad. On those tough days, remind yourself of these affirmations:

- "It's okay to not be okay."
- "My feelings are valid, no matter how messy."
- "I'm doing the best I can, and that's enough."

When the mess feels too overwhelming, remember that seeking help is okay. Talking to a friend, joining a support group, or finding a counselor can provide a lifeline. Sometimes, sharing the mess can help lighten the load.

Your grief might be messy, but within that mess, there's a testament to your love, resilience, and capacity to navigate through the most challenging times. When the waves hit, let them come. Cry over the kitchen sink, laugh until you cry, and remember, through it all, you're not alone. Grief might be a mess, but it's our mess, and we'll get through it—one messy, unpredictable day at a time.

Why You Have to Let It Out

id you ever carry a backpack to school, filled to the top with heavy textbooks, notebooks, pencils, pens, etc.? Do you remember how heavy that felt? In grief, that backpack is full of emotions. We lug it around, day in and day out, adding more weight with every memory and every trigger until the backpack is about to burst at the seams and our back is about to break from the weight. Sometimes, without even realizing it, we start avoiding what's in that backpack because, let's face it, facing those emotions head-on can feel like opening Pandora's box. But here's the thing: avoiding these feelings doesn't lighten the load. It does the opposite.

Feeling Avoidance

How do we sidestep these emotions? Oh, we are a creative bunch, aren't we?! We throw ourselves into work, becoming the poster children for overtime. Or we work on building our husband's dream patio until it's too dark to wield a hammer. We binge-watch TV shows, letting fictional worlds blur the edges of our reality. I'm glad that wasn't a thing in the 1990s. Or maybe I'm projecting again. We might even pick up new hobbies at breakneck speed, anything to keep our minds occupied. And then there's the classic: plastering on a smile and insisting we're "fine" when friends and family ask how we're holding up. It's not that we're trying to lie to them or ourselves; it's just that diving into the messiness of our grief feels too daunting.

Unhealthy Avoidance

At first glance, this dance around our feelings might seem a harmless, temporary fix. But the truth is, it comes with a cost, just like when we talked about denial. Physically, our bodies are on high alert, constantly bracing for the impact of emotions we're not letting ourselves feel. This can lead to sleepless nights, a heart that races for no apparent reason, and a general sense of being unwell. Mentally, it's like we're building a dam to hold back a river; the pressure keeps mounting, and if we're not careful, it can crack, leading to outbursts that surprise even us. The energy it takes to dodge these emotions can leave us feeling drained, robbing us of the chance to find genuine peace and healing moments.

Benefits of Venting

So, what happens when we finally unzip that backpack and start unpacking it? At first, it's going to feel like taking a deep breath after being underwater for too long. Expressing our grief by letting those emotions flow can be incredibly relieving. It's acknowledging that, yes, we're hurting, and that's okay. This venting can take many forms: talking with someone we trust, crying in the shower, or even screaming into a pillow. It's all valid. The relief from venting isn't just emotional; it's also physical. Our sleep improves, our appetite might come back, and that constant feeling of being on edge starts to fade. We begin to find clarity amidst the chaos, discovering what we truly need to move through our grief.

I remember one day at work, my co-worker Rose asked if I was doing okay. I looked at her, my eyes bloodshot from drinking too much the night before or crying moments ago (either reason would be accurate), "Do you want the truth, or are you just asking to be polite?" I'd run out of politeness, opting for an answer other than, "I'm fine."

"I'll take the truth," she bravely answered. "I don't want to do this anymore," I told her. I wept at work, finally letting some of it out.

Release Techniques

After avoiding and hiding my emotions behind a bottle for a while, I learned that finding healthy ways to let out these emotions is vital. Here are a few techniques that can help:

- **Talking it Out**: Sometimes, a good, old-fashioned chat is the best release. Talking about what you're going through can be incredibly cathartic, whether it's a friend, a family member, or a therapist. Tears might be part of this, and that's okay.
- **Creative Expression**: For those who find words insufficient or too direct, channeling your emotions into something creative can be a powerful outlet. Painting, writing, playing music—these activities let you express your grief in ways that words cannot. I had a hard time sharing my emotions with others... what does a 28-year-old know about grieving their dead husband? As a way for me to work through my feelings and to adequately share them, I mentioned creating a series of mixtapes sharing my journey. Then I wrote. Then I acted.
- **Physical Activity**: Physical movement can be a great way to release pent-up emotions. Whether it's a brisk walk, a run, or punching a bag in kickboxing, movement helps release endorphins. Those are the feel-good hormones that can lift our spirits and help us cope.

- **Mindfulness and Meditation**: These practices can help us sit with our emotions without judgment, acknowledging them as they come and go. It's not about avoiding or suppressing feelings but about letting them exist within us, giving us a sense of peace and acceptance.

Letting out our grief, giving voice to our pain, and letting tears flow when they need to is not a sign of weakness. It's a brave step toward healing. It's recognizing that to carry on, we sometimes need to stop, set down that heavy backpack, and sort through what's inside. In these moments of release, we find strength we didn't know we had, and slowly, we start to feel a little lighter, a little more ready to face the days ahead.

Negative Emotions

E very day, we're confronted with emotions, and while grieving, many of them magnify and swirl around us like a relentless storm, each one touching us with a different intensity. It's crucial to understand that emotions, in and of themselves, carry no moral weight. They are neither inherently good nor bad. Their impact on us and how they shape our journey through grief lends them significance. Each emotion we encounter in grief is complex, multifaceted, and deeply intertwined with our unique experiences of loss. Still, let's talk about some of the significant "negative" emotions we encounter that may prevent us from healing.

Sadness
Sadness often stands at the forefront of grief; it's a deep, engulfing wave that can carry us into the depths of despair. Sadness is not only natural; it's necessary. It signifies the depth of our bonds and the love we have for what we've lost. Allowing ourselves to feel sadness is a crucial step in the healing process. Expressing this emotion can be as simple as crying when the need strikes or sharing our feelings with someone who understands. Sometimes, writing letters to what or whom we've lost can provide a tangible outlet for our despair, a way to articulate the inarticulable.

Despair
Unchecked, however, sadness can lead to despair and a complete loss of hope. When you find no meaning in life, destructive behaviors take place. In *Life After Losses,* I wrote at length about how I found myself in this dark place for two years

before finally breaking free. Despair can be a destructive force casting a pall over the possibility of recovery or positive change. Unchecked, despair can lead to a cycle of negative thinking and emotional paralysis, making it difficult to see beyond current hardships and toward potential solutions or brighter days ahead.

Anger

You may find yourself angry at yourself, or your loved one, or the doctor, or the EMT, or the … you fill in the blank. Anger is normal while grieving, but it often catches us off guard. It's a reaction to the unfairness of loss; it protests a reality we did not choose. Understanding that this anger is a normal response to feeling powerless can help us navigate it healthily. Channeling this intense emotion into activities like physical exercise or creative expression can provide a release, transforming it from destructive fire into a source of strength and motivation.

Guilt/Shame

Guilt and shame often burrow their way into grief. They're the shadowy figures that whisper in our minds of what we could have done differently. These emotions feed on our insecurities, on the painful scrutiny of hindsight. Recognizing that guilt and shame are often grounded in our love and care for the departed can help us approach them compassionately. Practices like writing down our guilt and *challenging* those feelings with facts and forgiveness can lighten their hold on us. It's about making peace with the fact that we did the best we could with the knowledge and resources we had at the time.

Relief

Relief is one emotion that dares not speak its name in the context of grief. Yet, feeling relief after a loss, especially following a prolonged illness or suffering, is more common than many admit. Acknowledging this sense of relief doesn't diminish our love or respect for the departed; it reflects our human capacity for empathy, wishing for an end to their suffering, and sometimes ours as caregivers. Understanding that relief can coexist with sorrow and loss allows us to embrace the full spectrum of our emotions without judgment.

Apathy

Apathy, or emotional numbness, is a void where we feel detached from the world and ourselves. This numbness is a defense mechanism, a way for our psyche to shield us from pain until we're ready to face it. Engaging in small, meaningful tasks or routines can gently coax us out of this state, reconnecting us with the world bit by bit. It's also helpful to set small, achievable goals that can bring a sense of accomplishment and purpose back into our lives.

Loneliness

Loneliness in grief is not just about being physically alone; it's a deep sense of isolation that comes from feeling that no one truly understands our loss. Combating this loneliness involves reaching out, even when it feels impossible. Connecting with support groups, whether in person or online, can provide a sense of community and understanding. Sometimes, simply being in the presence of others, even without talking about our grief, can remind us that we're not as isolated as we feel.

You Are Not Alone

Grief is a maze with its twists and turns of complex emotions, and it's easy to feel lost, to believe that we're navigating this path alone. But remember these emotions—sadness, despair, anger, guilt/shame, relief, apathy, and loneliness—are universal signposts of the grieving process. They know no boundaries. They remind us that we're part of a broader human experience, connected by the very emotions that seem to isolate us. Recognizing that others have walked this path and felt these emotions can be a source of comfort and strength. It's a reminder that, no matter how solitary our journey through grief might seem, we are, in truth, surrounded by a silent chorus of shared understanding and empathy.

Self-Forgiveness: Healing the Wounds of What Ifs and If Onlys

Navigating through grief often feels like walking through a hall of funhouse mirrors, each reflection distorting a version of ourselves haunted by guilt and regret. The echoes of what-ifs and if-onlys can be deafening, creating a cacophony of self-blame that makes cicadas sound quiet. Yet it's in the heart of this maze of mirrors where we find the key to liberation: self-forgiveness. This isn't about absolving ourselves of imagined faults but acknowledging our human limitations and extending kindness to ourselves, just as we would to a dear friend.

While it sounds easy, forgiving ourselves is far from a straightforward task. It requires us to confront painful truths, to sit with the discomfort acknowledging our imperfections, and to accept that, despite our best efforts, outcomes beyond our control unfolded. Self-forgiveness is much like caring for a wound; it's delicate, demands patience, and, most importantly, is necessary for healing.

Addressing Guilt and Regret

Guilt and regret often stem from some belief that we could have acted differently, that somehow our actions or inactions contributed to our loss, and if only we'd done XYZ, they'd still be alive, or if we'd done ABC, the path would look different. To move past these feelings, we have to unpack them, laying them bare. Let's acknowledge some truth here:

- **Identify the Source**: Pinpoint exactly what you're feeling guilty or regretful about. Is it something you said, did, or perhaps something you wish you had done?
- **Challenge the Guilt**: Could you have honestly acted differently, given the information and emotional state you were in at the time? Remember, hindsight is 20/20.

Practicing Self-Forgiveness

Embracing self-forgiveness is a practice that requires repetition and dedication. It's easier to forgive others, but this needs to be about you. Here are a few ways you can do so:

- **Self-Compassion Exercises**: Treat yourself with the kindness you'd offer a loved one. Speak to yourself with understanding and compassion. Simple affirmations can be a starting point, reminders that you're doing your best.
- **Reframing Negative Thoughts**: When you catch yourself spiraling into guilt or regret, pause. Try to reframe these thoughts. Instead of "I should have," remind yourself, "I did what I thought was best at the time."

Letting Go of Burdens

The what-ifs and if-onlys are burdens we carry, often unconsciously. Letting them go isn't about forgetting or minimizing our feelings but about freeing ourselves from the weight of things we cannot change; it allows us to focus on the present and healing. Visualization can be a powerful tool:

- Close your eyes and imagine placing these burdens in a balloon and watching it float away. With each breath, visualize letting go a little more, feeling lighter with each release.

- Focus on your breath and the rise and fall of your chest. With each breath out, the balloon gets smaller and smaller until you can no longer see it.

Forgiveness as a Gift

Viewing self-forgiveness as a gift is a paradigm shift that can help on the path of healing. This gift isn't wrapped in ribbons; it's messy, hard-won, and precious. It's the permission to acknowledge our grief without the added weight of guilt. It's the realization that moving forward doesn't mean leaving behind but carrying with us the love and lessons learned, unencumbered by self-blame.

This gift of forgiveness is a crucial step in reclaiming our lives. It allows us to breathe a little easier and see the possibilities of a future where grief and joy coexist. It shows our resilience. It is a declaration that while grief may shape us, it does not define us.

The path to self-forgiveness is intensely personal; it's a journey made in small, often imperceptible steps. It's a path paved with patience, kindness, and an unwavering commitment to ourselves. Through self-forgiveness, we find healing, a renewed sense of freedom, a readiness to embrace the world with open hearts, and the courage to step into the next chapter of our lives, whatever it may hold.

Reflecting on Your PURPOSE Journal

When working on your PURPOSE Journal, remember the prompts for **Unload Your Emotional Baggage:** What are the feelings you're struggling with the most right now? Allow yourself to express them here without judgment.

Reflect upon what you've learned in this chapter and your feelings. Grab a pen and your journal or a piece of paper, and find a comfortable, serene spot where you can be uninterrupted. Take a moment to breathe deeply, centering yourself, and preparing your heart and mind for this journey inward. We're going to spend some time just focusing on our emotions.

- What emotions have you felt today? How intense were they, on a scale of one to ten? How did you cope (or not) with them? Sadness, despair, anger, guilt/shame, relief, apathy, loneliness, joy, dread, hope? Were there others?

In this chapter, we've explored the emotions that color our experience and the importance of extending kindness to ourselves through self-forgiveness. This exploration helps us grow through our grief, discovering the strength within our vulnerability and the beauty within our pain. As we continue on this journey, let's carry the lessons of self-compassion and the transformative power of forgiveness forward.

Chapter 4: *R*each Out for Support

"Refusing to ask for help when you need it is refusing someone the chance to be helpful." ~ Ric Ocasek

Imagine grief as a dense fog. It's easy to feel lost, to lose sight of the path ahead and even the ground beneath your feet. Now, think about what happens when a lighthouse beam cuts through that fog. Suddenly, you're not just wandering; you have a direction, a beacon to guide you. This is what community can be in the midst of grief: a light guiding us back to ourselves and each other, showing us that even in our darkest moments, we aren't alone. I learned after my first loss that I shouldn't have pushed people away, but I was so wrapped up in my own pain without the tools or emotional maturity to know better. I later learned that in doing so, I deprived others who wished to be of service, and that wasn't fair to them or supporting their needs.

The Importance of Community in Grief Recovery

Community Support
The power of community support during grief recovery can't be overstated. Sometimes, it's a formal support group led by a professional. Other times, it's an online community of strangers or a network of friends and family. Each provides a unique kind of comfort. Imagine someone else articulating the whirlwind of emotions you couldn't quite put into words. There's an immediate sense of relief, isn't there? It's like finding a clearing in the woods, a space where the fog lifts, and you can breathe easier knowing someone else gets it.

Shared Experiences
Hearing others share their stories of loss and grief is grounding and uplifting. It's a reminder that grief, in all its forms, is a universal human experience. The value here isn't just in knowing you're not alone; it's in seeing how other people cope, heal, and honor their loved ones. These stories can be a source of inspiration, a collection of luminarias lighting a path you might not have seen on your own. I often tell people to use my path as inspiration in their journey toward healing but not to follow it. I figured if I could make it, maybe my story could help.

Active Participation
Getting involved with these communities isn't just about finding support; it's also about giving it. Supporting others in their grief can strengthen your own recovery. It reminds you that you're resilient and strong even when you're at your most

vulnerable. Whether sharing your story, offering a listening ear, or simply being present, your participation adds another candle to the footpath luminarias guiding your community through the fog.

Building Your Circle
Finding the right community for your needs is crucial. But how do you find it?

- **Identify What You Need**: Do you want a space to share openly, or do you prefer to listen and learn from others' experiences? Your needs can guide which community will suit you best.
- **Explore Options**: Look into local support groups, search for online communities, or consider starting a small group with friends or family who understand your loss.
- **Give It Time**: Finding the right fit might take a few tries, and that's okay. The important thing is not to rush. Allow yourself to find a space where you feel understood and supported.
- **Contribute**: Once you've found a community that feels right, think about how you can contribute. Sometimes, the simple act of showing up is enough.

Finding strength in each other is about more than just shared experiences; it's about building a network of understanding and empathy. It's about creating that support system that holds us up when we struggle to stand. It's about transforming what feels like our solitary journey of grief into a shared voyage toward healing, where every story and every gesture of support adds to the group's collective strength. In this community, every member, including you, is guiding and being guided through the fog of grief toward a place of hope and renewal.

Some may say you can walk this path alone, but I caution that the alone path is far more difficult. Grieving is hard enough, and having support can be crucial to your healing.

The Different Kinds of Support Out There

When you find yourself seeking additional support, you're not admitting defeat. You're acknowledging the courage it takes to do so. If you find your thoughts consumed by loss to the point where days blend into nights with little difference, or if the joy in activities that once brought happiness has dimmed, these might be signals it's time to reach out. Recognizing that the weight of grief is not a burden to carry alone is crucial. There's absolutely nothing wrong with seeking professional help; it's a proactive step toward reassembling the puzzle pieces after grief throws them on the floor.

Bereavement Support

There's a slew of bereavement support available to you, with each option offering its unique form of comfort and understanding. You may find one or more of these helpful in different ways. Here's a glance at the variety:

- **Individual Therapy**: Offers a one-on-one setting with a therapist specializing in grief, providing a personalized approach to healing.
- **Support Groups**: These are gatherings, either in person or online, where individuals share their experiences of loss, fostering a sense of community and shared understanding.
- **Workshops and Seminars**: Often led by experts in grief recovery, these sessions provide educational resources on coping mechanisms and healing practices.
- **Online Forums and Social Media Groups**: Digital spaces where individuals can share anonymously, offering

flexibility and accessibility to those who may not be ready for face-to-face interactions.

Each support system serves a unique purpose in the healing process, catering to different needs and comfort levels. Now that you know several types, how do you choose what's right for you? I've attempted to share some pros and cons to help you decide.

Pros and Cons
Navigating through the options requires weighing their benefits and limitations:

- **Individual Therapy**
  - *Pros*: Tailored support; privacy; focus on individual needs.
  - *Cons*: Cost may be prohibitive for some; finding the right therapist can take time.
- **Support Groups**
  - *Pros*: Sense of community; understanding that you're not alone; diverse perspectives and coping strategies.
  - *Cons*: Group settings may be intimidating for some; discussions can trigger emotional responses.
- **Workshops and Seminars**
  - *Pros*: Access to expert advice; structured learning environment; resources for further reading and practice.
  - *Cons*: Less personalized; may not address individual emotional needs directly.

- **Online Forums and Social Media Groups**
  - *Pros*: Anonymity; accessible anytime; wide range of experiences and advice.
  - *Cons*: Risk of misinformation; lack of professional moderation in some forums.

Finding the Right Support

Discovering the support system that resonates with your journey involves a few steps:

- **Reflect on Your Needs**: Start by asking what you're looking for in a support system. Is it understanding, advice, shared experiences, or just a space to express your feelings? Your answer will direct you toward the correct type of support, just as with your community circle.
- **Research**: Dive into the options available in your area or online. Look for participant reviews or testimonials to gauge the effectiveness of different support systems.
- **Trial and Error**: It's okay to try a few options before finding the one that feels right. Whether it's a therapist, a support group, or an online community, the fit is crucial to your comfort and openness in sharing your grief.
- **Ask for Recommendations**: Sometimes, the best way to find support is through the advice of others who have walked a similar path. Don't hesitate to contact friends, family, or even healthcare professionals for suggestions.

No matter which you choose, each choice is a path to healing. Some options may resonate more deeply with your personal needs, while others provide quiet support. The journey of selecting the right mix is personal, focusing on self-awareness, recognizing your progress, and adapting your support as you work through grief's stages. Again, I feel it's important to remind you that seeking help is a sign of strength, not weakness. It shows your resolve to move through grief toward peace.

Asking for Help

I'm a reasonably self-sufficient adult; that's how my Mom raised me, so I have difficulty asking for help. The idea of reaching out for help while deep in grief can stir your emotions, from vulnerability to fear of rejection. I found facing this challenge was a pivotal step toward healing, not because it's simple (it wasn't), but due to its impact on my path to recovery.

Understanding the Hurdle

The act of asking for help goes beyond admitting that we can't manage everything alone; it touches on the essence of our vulnerability. We're already hurting; who wants to be more vulnerable? This vulnerability reflects our humanity, reminding us that we're all interconnected in the grand scheme of life. We're reliant on the others for strength and support. However, societal norms often prize self-reliance, telling us that strength excludes the act of reaching out. This expectation can make the decision to ask for help feel like stepping into uncharted territory, marked by the fear of being seen as incapable or becoming a burden to others.

Pinpointing Your Needs

Before you can ask for help, it's crucial to identify what form of help you need. Especially in the early months, grief can cloud our ability to see what we need most, so taking the time to think about what you really need is important. Consider categorizing your needs into broader umbrellas such as:

- **Personal**: Emotional support, someone to listen to you, or companionship for moments when solitude weighs heavily.
- **Household**: Assistance with daily chores, meals, or managing routine tasks that seem overwhelming. I didn't cook for at least two months after my second husband died.
- **Financial**: Guidance on managing expenses, understanding potential benefits, or navigating paperwork that accompanies loss.
- **Grief**: Helping find spaces where you can share your feelings openly, whether through counseling, support groups, or one-on-one conversations with those who've walked similar paths.
- **Well-Being**: Encouraging reminders to care for your physical health, be it through exercise, nutrition, or rest.

Crafting Your Approach

Once you've defined your needs, the next step is to effectively communicate them. Here are some strategies to consider:

- **Choose the Right Moment**: Look for a time when you and the person you're reaching out to aren't rushed. A calm, private setting can foster a more meaningful conversation.
- **Be Direct but Flexible**: Clearly express what you need, but remain open to how others might be able to help. Sometimes, they might offer support in ways you hadn't considered.
- **Express Appreciation**: Acknowledge that their support is valuable and appreciated. Gratitude not only reinforces

your connection but can make helping mutually rewarding.

- **Reciprocate**: While your ability to offer support might be limited during this time, expressing your willingness to reciprocate when able can strengthen the bonds of mutual aid.

Initiating the Conversation

Here's a template to guide your request for help, adaptable to your specific needs:

1. **Start with Gratitude**: "I really appreciate you taking the time to listen. Your support means a lot to me."
2. **State Your Need**: "I've been finding it hard to [specific need], and I could use some help."
3. **Specify the Help You Seek**: "It would really help me if [specific action]."
4. **Acknowledge Their Effort**: "I understand everyone has their commitments, so any assistance you can offer would be greatly appreciated."

Remember, the responses you receive might vary, and that's okay. People will often be more willing and able to help than you anticipate, but their ability to provide support can differ based on their circumstances. Your worth is not tied to any response.

Asking for help is a way to gather the resources you need to navigate this challenging path. It's a sign that you're moving toward a place where the fog begins to clear, allowing glimpses of the landscape ahead—a landscape marked by healing, connection, and renewed strength.

Maintaining a Supportive Network

In the wake of loss, the dynamics of our relationships inevitably shift. Friends and family, who were once distant, might draw closer, eager to offer their support. On the other hand, those we expected to lean on might suddenly seem absent, probably unsure of how to navigate our grief's complex waters. In some cases, I lost family; in others, I lost friends (especially coupled friends). Still, in others, I found friends who became my chosen family. It's a period marked by change, not just internally but also in our social lives. Nurturing these evolving relationships requires patience, openness, and some strategy.

Relationships Change

The dynamics of relationships in grief are intricate. What used to be a simple connection may now carry new layers of emotion and expectation. It's crucial to remember that everyone processes grief differently, and these differences can affect how people relate to you and your loss, as well as how *you* relate to others and *their* loss. Here's how to keep the bonds strong:

- **Communicate Your Needs**: People aren't mind readers. What you need from your relationships might have changed, and it's okay to voice these new needs.
- **Allow Space**: Just as you are navigating your grief, so are those around you. Giving each other space to process can prevent feelings of suffocation and frustration.
- **Reset Expectations**: Acknowledge that your relationships might not return to "how things were." That's not necessarily a bad thing; it's an opportunity to build deeper, more meaningful connections.

- **Be Forgiving**: Missteps will happen. Friends might say the wrong thing, not out of malice but out of a genuine desire to help. Holding onto forgiveness can prevent these moments from driving wedges in your relationships.

Mastering the Art of Opening Up

Sharing your grief isn't about unloading your emotions onto someone else; it's about inviting them into your experience and allowing them to walk beside you. Here's how you can open up effectively:

- **Choose the Right Listener**: Not everyone will be equipped to support you in the way you need. Do you remember my story about Rose? I knew she was the right listener because I knew her, and I knew she was ready when she asked for the truth. Find those in your circle who can offer the level of empathy and understanding you're looking for.
- **Set the Scene**: Pick a time and place where you feel safe and won't be rushed. This can help make the conversation feel less daunting for you and the listener.
- **Use "I Feel" Statements**: Start your sentences with "I feel," as it centers the conversation around your experience and reduces the chance of the listener feeling defensive or overwhelmed.
- **Ask for What You Need**: If you want advice, say so. If you just need to vent, make that clear. Setting expectations helps both parties feel more comfortable with the exchange.

Grieving Together

Grief can feel like a solitary experience, and sometimes it is. But it doesn't have to be. Finding ways to grieve together, mostly with friends and family, can strengthen your support network and provide mutual healing. Consider these approaches:

- **Create Shared Rituals**: Whether lighting candles, sharing stories, or visiting a place that holds significance, shared rituals can offer comfort and connection.
- **Offer Mutual Support**: Be there for others in their moments of grief, just as they are for you. This reciprocity creates a web of support where everyone feels held and understood.
- **Acknowledge Their Grief**: Remember, you're not the only one grieving. Acknowledge the pain of those around you and find ways to support each other. Your wife was your mother-in-law's daughter.
- **Learn Together**: Explore resources on grief together. Books, workshops, and seminars can offer new perspectives and coping strategies that you can discuss and implement as a group.

Maintaining a supportive network is about finding balance, whether dealing with loss or not. It's about nurturing your relationships through open communication, mutual understanding, and shared experiences. As these connections evolve, they become pillars of support, not just for you but for everyone involved, creating a community where grief is acknowledged, shared, and, ultimately, part of the larger story of your lives together.

Reflecting on Your PURPOSE Journal

W hen working on your PURPOSE Journal, remember your **Reach Out for Support** prompts: Who did you connect with today, or who can you reach out to tomorrow for support? What kind of support do you need the most right now (listening ear, distraction, advice)? Additionally, reflect on any support you may have provided others.

Reflect upon what you've learned in this chapter and your feelings. Grab a pen and your journal or a piece of paper, and find a comfortable, serene spot where you can be uninterrupted. Take a moment to breathe deeply, centering yourself, and preparing your heart and mind for this journey inward. Right now, we want to focus on your support system.

Creating a support system is like building a raft that will help you navigate off the deserted island. We will start making a guide to assembling that raft, piece by piece, ensuring it's sturdy enough to carry you through. It's about recognizing the materials you have at your disposal—the people, activities, and resources that can buoy you when the waves seem insurmountable. Think more of *Cast Away* than *Gilligan's Island*.

Identifying Key Supporters

Start by listing the individuals in your life who have supported you in the past. Think about why each person has been significant. What specific qualities or actions made their support meaningful? This could range from a friend who's always ready to listen to a family member who helps with day-to-day tasks or even a colleague like Rose who's offered a shoulder to lean on. Recognize that support can come from unexpected places and that sometimes, those who haven't experienced grief can still provide substantial support through empathy and willingness to help. Think of

- Friends
- Family members
- Colleagues
- Professionals (therapists, counselors)
- Community members

Support Activities

Next, reflect on activities that bring you comfort or a sense of peace. These can be simple actions like taking a walk, engaging in a hobby, or attending a support group meeting. Activities that connect you with others or allow for reflective solitude can be vital components of your support system. Write down a few activities you feel could be beneficial to bring into your routine, noting how often and in what context you might engage in them. Note if you can do these alone or with others and how you'd prefer to do so. For example, you could walk alone in the countryside or join a hiking group, which would you prefer? Here are a few more examples:

- Walking in nature
- Journaling or creative writing
- Artistic pursuits (painting, drawing, crafting)
- Engaging in sports or physical exercise
- Attending support group sessions

Resources and Tools

Consider the resources and tools that could help in your healing process. These might include books on grief, online forums, podcasts, or therapeutic tools like meditation apps. List resources you've found helpful or ones you're interested in exploring. If you're uncertain where to start, ask for recommendations from your support network or professionals. Your list may include some of these:

- Grief-related books
- Meditation or mindfulness apps
- Supportive podcasts
- Online forums or social media groups
- Professional services (therapy, counseling)

Making Connections

Now, draw lines connecting the supporters, activities, and resources that align or complement each other. For instance, a friend who enjoys hiking can be linked to your interest in walking in nature, or a family member who's also exploring grief might be connected to a book or podcast you've found insightful. This visual mapping can help you see the potential synergies within your support system, making it easier to reach out and make plans that reinforce your support network.

Action Plan

With your support system mapped out, create a simple action plan. Start small, choosing one or two steps you feel ready to take. This could be as straightforward as scheduling a weekly walk with a friend or joining a local or online support group. Write down what you need to do to initiate each action, and give yourself a deadline to encourage follow-through. Building a support system is a gradual process; every step forward is a positive move toward healing. Your action plan could feature things like this:

- Schedule a weekly walk with a friend.
- Join an online grief support forum.
- Borrow a recommended book on grief from the library.
- Download a meditation app and explore beginner sessions.

Obviously, this isn't a one-and-done exercise. As you move through your grief, your needs and the support available to you will evolve. Return to this as often as needed, adding new supporters, activities, and resources as you discover them. Your support system is a living entity that grows and changes just as you do. Personally, I find visual mapping to be beneficial.

In wrapping up this chapter, I want to make sure you know it's vital to recognize that while grief can feel isolating, you are surrounded by a myriad of support options waiting to be tapped into. From the people in your life who care deeply about you to the activities that offer comfort and the wealth of resources available, you have the pieces to construct a raft-like support system that can hold you steady through the storm. As you turn the page to the next chapter, carry the knowledge that you're not navigating this path alone. Though challenging, your raft is well-equipped, and your journey toward healing is supported by a network of love and understanding.

A Call to Kindness
Impact a Stranger's Life with Your Words

"We cannot take away their grief, but we can walk beside them." –
Unknown

D id you know? People who give without wanting anything in return tend to lead longer, happier lives and even end up making more money.

Now, I've got a special question for you...

Would you be willing to help someone you've never met, even if you knew you'd never get a "thank you" for it?

Who is this mysterious person, you might wonder? Well, they're a bit like you. Maybe not as familiar with the twists and turns of life, wanting to find support and heal, but unsure of where to find it.

Our big goal is to make the journey of grief recovery for adults something anyone can embark on. Everything I do is driven by this goal. To achieve it, I need to reach, well, ...basically everyone.

This is where your superpower comes into play. Yes, it's true that a lot of folks decide on a book by its cover (and what others say about it), right? So, on behalf of that person grappling with loss whom you've never met, here's my heartfelt request:

Please consider leaving a review for this book.

This small act of kindness doesn't cost a dime and takes just a moment, yet it has the power to profoundly impact someone else's life. Your review might be the beacon of hope that helps...

...one more individual find peace in their community.
...one more person rebuild their life.
...one more soul discover meaningful connections.
...and maybe, just maybe, turn one more dream into reality.

Feeling that 'warm and fuzzy' inside and ready to make a real difference? And it takes less than 60 seconds of your time to:

Leave a review.

Just scan the QR code below to share your thoughts:

If the idea of helping someone out there in the world lights up your day, then you're precisely the kind of person I was hoping to find. Welcome to the club—you're one of the good ones.

I'm even more excited to help you discover your new direction and purpose than you could imagine. The strategies that are coming your way are something special.

A huge thank you from the deepest part of my heart. Now, let's start looking at what the future holds for you.

Your biggest cheerleader,
James LaVeck

P.S. Fun fact: Sharing something valuable with someone else benefits them and increases your worth in their eyes. If you believe this book could be a lifeline for another individual navigating grief and you want to spread some goodwill, why not pass it along to them?

Chapter 5: *P*robe for Personal Significance

"How lucky I am to have something that makes saying goodbye so hard." ~ A. A. Milne

Imagine standing at the base of a towering mountain. Its peak, shrouded in mist, seems insurmountable. Now, picture yourself taking a few steps to the side. The mountain's shape changes, the path up becomes more apparent, and what once seemed an impossible climb now appears a challenging but navigable journey. This shift in perspective, this slight change in position, transforms the entire landscape. It's a powerful metaphor for how altering our viewpoint can significantly impact our approach to and experience of grief.

Mindset: The Lens Through Which We View Grief

O ur mindset acts as the lens through which we interpret the world around us, coloring our experiences, reactions, and emotions. In the throes of grief, it's easy for this lens to become clouded, to view our loss as that insurmountable mountain casting a long shadow over every aspect of our lives. However, by consciously adjusting this lens and shifting our mindset, we can begin to see our grief in a different light.

Consider the difference between saying, "I have to get through this day" versus "I get to live this day." The former carries a weight of obligation, a hurdle to clear; the latter implies a gift, an opportunity. This subtle shift in language demonstrates how a change in mindset can significantly influence how we navigate our grief.

Embracing a Transformative Perspective: "Because Of"

Moving from an "in spite of" to a "because of" mindset can be a transformative process in grief recovery. "In spite of" implies a battle, a struggle against grief, where every day is about pushing back, resisting, and surviving in spite of the pain. It's exhausting and can make us feel like we're constantly defending against our emotions.

On the other hand, adopting a "because of" mindset means recognizing that our grief, while a source of immense pain, can also be a catalyst for growth, change, and new understandings. It's about finding ways to grow not just *in spite of* our loss but *because of* it. This doesn't mean the pain is any less real or the loss any less significant. Instead, it's about acknowledging that our experiences of loss and grief can lead to profound insights about ourselves, our relationships, and our world.

- For someone who's lost a partner, it might mean discovering a strength and independence they never knew they had.
- A parent dealing with the unimaginable grief of losing a child might find a new purpose in advocating for causes their child cared about.
- Someone bereaved might take up a hobby or interest that their loved one enjoyed, finding connection and solace in the activity.

Consider these examples:

	In Spite Of	**Because of**
	Isolation	**Connection**
Feeling	Because of my grief, I understand the value of connecting with others who have experienced similar experiences.	
	Avoidance	**Engagement**
Action	Because of my loss, I want to engage in activities that keep my loved one's memory alive.	
	Stagnation	**Growth**
Healing	Because of my grief, I've gained a deeper understanding of myself and what matters to me.	
	Despair	**Meaning**
Perspective	Because of my grief, I've discovered new purposes and directions in my life.	
	Loss of Self	**Rediscovery**
Identity	Because of my grief, I am learning who I am in this new chapter of my life.	

How Mindset Can Heal

The power of a shifted perspective in healing from grief cannot be overstated. Studies in the field of positive psychology show that individuals who can find meaning or a sense of purpose in the face of adversity are more likely to experience less intense grief and to find a renewed sense of life satisfaction over time. This isn't about putting a positive spin on our pain or denying the depths of our sorrow. It's not about toxic positivity or perpetual Pollyana-ism. Instead, it's about opening ourselves up to the possibility that there are opportunities for learning, growth, and even joy within our grief. Sometimes, we just need to get out of our own way.

Here are a few strategies for cultivating this mindset:

- **Reflect on Changes**: Regularly take time to reflect on how your grief has changed you. What have you learned about yourself? How have your relationships shifted? What new understandings have you gained about what truly matters in life?
- **Set Intentions**: Each morning, set an intention for the day that reflects your "because of" mindset. It could be as simple as "Today, I choose to find joy in small moments" or "Today, I honor my loved one by living fully."
- **Practice Gratitude**: Even on the most challenging days, try to identify one thing you're grateful for. Over time, this practice can help shift your focus from what you've lost to what you still have.

Finding the "Good" in "Goodbye"

Under the layers of grief, hidden amongst the sorrow and loss, lies a seed of something transformative. It's not easily found and often goes unnoticed until we're ready to look for it. This is the essence of finding the "good" in "goodbye." It's about recognizing that while grief is a response to loss, it also holds the potential to lead us to great discoveries about ourselves and the world around us.

A Deeper Meaning

When we sift through the remnants of what we've lost, we might discover insights and understandings we certainly didn't anticipate. These aren't just reflections on the past but glimpses of how we can live in the future. For example, the loss of a loved one can deepen our sense of empathy, making us more attuned to the struggles of others. Or, it can sharpen our appreciation for life's fragility, prompting us to live more fully and with greater intention. The key is to allow ourselves the space to explore these insights, let them surface naturally, and recognize them as valuable perspectives. They're not replacements for what we've lost but rather growths that stem from our experience of loss, much like the new growth after a fire.

Making Space in Your Heart

Making room for happiness in the wake of grief might seem impossible, and I would have argued it impossible had I not found it not only possible but attainable. It can even feel like a betrayal of what or whom we've lost. But here's a thought: allowing joy back into our lives honors our loved ones by living as fully as they would have wanted us to. I feel I honor them by living the life they couldn't. This doesn't mean the pain of loss disappears or that we forget. No, it means we allow ourselves to experience joy alongside our sorrow. This could start small—a moment of laughter, a smile at a fond memory, or the sun's warmth on your face. These slivers of happiness don't diminish the depth of our grief; they coexist with it, reminding us that the capacity for joy is as much a part of us as our capacity for sorrow. This is a lesson learned about life; both can coexist.

How Grief Changes You for the Better

It's a delicate balance, talking about the ways grief can lead to personal growth without romanticizing the pain that caused it. The truth is that grief is a catalyst for change. It can push us to re-evaluate our priorities, deepen our connections with others, and pursue paths we might have hesitated to explore before. This growth isn't a silver lining of loss; it's a statement about our ability to adapt, to find resilience within ourselves, and to seek meaning in the aftermath of sorrow. It's about recognizing that while grief might shape us, it also allows us to reshape ourselves in response.

Your Loss Does Not Define You

In the narrative of our lives, loss is a chapter, not the entire book. Yes, it's a significant, life-altering chapter, but it's not where our story ends. We are more than our grief. We are the sum of all our experiences, relationships, and choices—both before and after our loss. Acknowledging our loss without letting it define us means recognizing its impact on our lives while embracing all the other factors that make us who we are. It's about holding space for our grief without letting it occupy all the space, allowing us to move forward with a sense of wholeness and self-awareness.

Finding the "good" in "goodbye" isn't about trivializing or diminishing the reality of our pain or the significance of our loss. It's about acknowledging that within the complex, often painful experience of grief are sparks of hope, resilience, and understanding that, when taken together, can lead us to a place of deeper compassion, appreciation, and purpose. It's a process that unfolds in its own time and way. But by making space for this exploration, by allowing ourselves to see beyond the immediate shadow of our loss, we open ourselves to a spectrum of experiences and emotions that enrich our lives in unexpected ways.

Rediscovering Joy & Gratitude: Small Steps Toward Pleasure

After a loss, the world can appear less bright, and seeking joy might seem as futile as trying to light a candle in a heavy rain. However, it is precisely in these times, in the subtle, unnoticed moments I refer to as the "in-between places," that we discover the enduring beauty of the world. This journey isn't about overshadowing our grief but recognizing that sorrow and happiness can coexist. This delicate balance doesn't lessen our loss. It pays tribute to the complexity of our emotions, showing us that experiencing joy amidst sorrow is not only possible but necessary for embracing life, even as we carry our loved ones in our hearts. This is the essence of *Life After Losses* and all I've tried to share over the years.

Finding Joy and Gratitude in the Everyday

The first glimpse of morning light, the aroma of freshly brewed coffee, the comforting weight of a book in your hands, the pet rubbing up against you—joy can be found in the simplest of things, waiting quietly for us to notice. Many times, it's about being present in the moment when we allow ourselves to fully experience and appreciate these everyday pleasures. Here's how you might start finding these little sparks of light:

- **Morning Routine**: Begin your day by identifying one thing you look forward to, no matter how small. It could be watching the sunrise, enjoying a quiet breakfast, snuggling with your pet, or listening to your favorite song.

- **Nature's Embrace**: Spend time in nature. Walking in the park or sitting in your garden can reconnect you with the cycle of life and growth, offering a serene backdrop where joy can flourish. You may find a butterfly tickling your nose or a hummingbird chirping near your ear.
- **Savor the Senses**: Make it a point to savor experiences through your senses. Relish the taste of your meals, immerse yourself in the textures of the world around you, and let the colors of your environment fill you with warmth.
- **Write in your PURPOSE Journal**: Write down something you're grateful for each night. They don't have to be significant or life-changing. Writing helps solidify these feelings, making them more tangible and accessible.

To help bring gratitude into your daily life, consider adding some of these exercises into your routine:

- **Gratitude Walks**: Take regular walks where your only purpose is to identify things you're grateful for. This could be the beauty of the trees, the feel of the sun on your skin, or the simple act of movement.
- **Gratitude Visits**: Think of someone who has positively impacted your life. Write them a letter expressing your gratitude, then, if possible, visit them to read the letter aloud. This act can strengthen bonds and spread the warmth of gratitude.
- **Gratitude Reflection**: At least once a week, set aside time to reflect on what you're grateful for. This can be through meditation, prayer, or simply quiet contemplation. Focus on feeling the gratitude in your body, letting it fill you with warmth and light.

New Hobbies and Interests

Exploring new hobbies or revisiting past interests can be a gateway to rediscovering pleasure. These activities provide a diversion and can become sources of fulfillment and joy. Whether painting, gardening, or learning to play an instrument, engaging in hobbies offers a productive outlet for emotions and a step toward healing. I took up so many things I didn't leave much time for myself and self-care, so while looking at new hobbies and interests, don't forget to take care of yourself. Consider these steps:

- **Trial and Exploration**: Allow yourself the freedom to try new things without the pressure of mastery. The goal is to explore and see what resonates with you. Explore the great, big world that's out there.
- **Connect with Others**: Join classes or groups related to your interest. This can be a way to meet new people, share your experiences, and find joy in shared activities.
- **Set Small Goals**: Set yourself small, achievable goals within your hobby. This can provide a sense of accomplishment and remind you of your ability to find joy and success in new endeavors.

Balancing Grief and Joy

Understanding that grief and joy can coexist is crucial. One does not invalidate the other. Instead, they weave together, forming the complex tapestry of human experience. Here are a few thoughts on maintaining this balance:

- **Give Yourself Permission**: Allow yourself to feel joy without guilt. It's okay to laugh, to have fun, and to enjoy moments of happiness. Your loved one won't mind.

- **Acknowledge Mixed Emotions**: It's normal to experience a range of emotions, sometimes simultaneously. Feeling joy does not mean you're forgetting your loss.
- **Embrace Moments of Happiness**: When you smile or laugh, embrace it. These moments of happiness are precious reminders that grief does not define your capacity for joy, and that's okay.

Celebrating Small Wins

Each step you take toward finding joy, no matter how small, is a victory. I've repeatedly reminded my son to take the win because life will eventually give you a loss. It's a sign of your resilience and your commitment to navigating life with openness and hope. Celebrate these moments:

- **Acknowledge Your Progress**: Take time to acknowledge your progress, whether engaging in a new hobby, finding joy in everyday moments, or simply getting through a tough day.
- **Share Your Wins**: Share these moments with friends or loved ones. Sharing can multiply your joy and encourage others on their own paths.
- **Reflect on Your Journey**: Add these small wins to your PURPOSE Journal, as we shared in Chapter Three. Looking back on your entries can be a powerful reminder of how far you've come and the moments of joy you've found along the way.

In this quiet pursuit of joy, though surrounded by grief, we learn that life is a mosaic of experiences—some painful, some beautiful, but all meaningful. In this realization, we find the strength to continue, open ourselves to the world in all its complexity, and embrace life's small pleasures. These steps toward joy are a part of our journey through grief, marked by growth, resilience, and the ever-present capacity for happiness.

Grieving Gratefully

The notion of grieving gratefully might seem paradoxical. Yet, it opens a path to a deeper, more nuanced understanding of our loss. It's about finding gratitude not for the loss itself but for what the experience has brought into our lives—strength we didn't know we possessed, a deeper appreciation for the moments we had with our loved ones, and a connection to a broader community of those who've walked similar paths. I wrote an online guest article on this subject for *Grappling with Grief*, exploring how gratitude has shaped my grief journey, offering solace and perspective. The short version is that I needed the second loss to put the first in perspective, and I needed the first to prepare for the second. Once I had this epiphany while writing *Life After Losses*, I felt clearer and more at peace than I had in over 25 years. It's a reminder that even in our darkest moments, there are glimmers of light, moments of grace that remind us of the richness and complexity of life.

To practice grieving gratefully, consider these steps:

- **Acknowledge the Growth**: Reflect on how you've grown since your loss. What qualities have you developed? How has your perspective shifted?
- **Appreciate the Connections**: Think about the relationships that have been strengthened or formed due to your grief. Express gratitude for the support and love you've received.

- **Honor Your Loved One**: Find ways to express gratitude for the time and experiences you shared with your loved one. This might be through rituals, writing, or creative expression.

When we make room for gratitude, even as we navigate through our grief, it's like we're giving ourselves permission to experience life in all its complexity. It's about finding some type of harmony in the midst of everything life throws our way, recognizing the beauty that exists alongside the pain. This doesn't mean we ignore our hurt; instead, it acts like a gentle reminder that there's still love, beauty, and connections around us worth holding onto.

Reflecting on Your PURPOSE Journal

When you're working on your PURPOSE Journal, remember your prompts for **Probe for Personal Significance**: What did your loss teach you about what truly matters in life? Are there insights you gained today about your values or priorities? Where have you found gratitude, or have you?

Reflect upon what you've learned in this chapter and your feelings. Grab a pen and your journal or a piece of paper, and find a comfortable, serene spot where you can be uninterrupted. Take a moment to breathe deeply, centering yourself, and preparing your heart and mind for this journey inward. We will focus on some of the difficult questions about your loss.

As we deal with the waves of grief, we often encounter questions that don't have easy answers. Yet, within these questions, we find the keys to unlocking a deeper understanding of our grief, a more profound connection to our lost loved ones, and a more straightforward path toward healing.

Diving into these tough questions isn't just about hunting for answers. It's like opening the door to a deeper understanding of how we deal with loss, how we love, and how we live our lives. Sure, it can be a bit scary, but it's eye-opening at the same time, and it takes us to some really meaningful places. Even when it gets uncomfortable, what we find out is always worth it.

The Whys and What-Ifs

Wondering "why" our loss happened and asking ourselves why it hit us or our loved ones is totally normal. These whys can stick around in our thoughts, replaying over and over. And then there are the what-ifs—thinking about how things could have been different, imagining other paths we could have taken, or things we could have done. Finding concrete answers to these questions might not happen, but going through them is part of dealing with life's unpredictability and the fact that we can't control everything. It's about learning to be okay with not having all the answers.

- Have a "why" that keeps challenging you? Try writing it down. Next to it, scribble any thoughts or emotions that bubble up when you dwell on it.
- Is there a "what-if" you keep circling back to? Let yourself fully ponder this question, but then, try to steer your thoughts towards accepting things as they are now.

The How's

Figuring out "how" to press on after losing someone is a huge question. It covers the nitty-gritty of getting by day-to-day without our loved one and the deeper, emotional work of healing. "How can I feel happy again?" "How do I keep their spirit alive?" "How do I understand a world that now seems so changed?" There aren't universal answers to these, but as we search, we find our way through grief. We learn what helps us feel a bit better, what doesn't help at all, what eases the ache, and what brings it surging back.

- Pick a "how" question that resonates with you. Create a list of potential answers or actions you can take, no matter how small. This list can serve as a starting point for experimentation and exploration.

The Who's

Loss can fundamentally alter our sense of identity. "Who am I now that they're gone?" This question reflects the impact our loved ones have on our lives and how, in their absence, we might feel lost or adrift. It's a journey of self-discovery, discovering who we are in the context of our loss and learning to integrate this new sense of self with the person we were before.

- Reflect on how your loss has changed you. What new qualities or strengths have you discovered in yourself? How can these insights help you redefine your sense of self?

Diving into these tough questions, we're really taking a hard look inside ourselves, and yeah, it's tough but also healing. It's a path that leads us toward a deeper understanding of our grief, and to see how strong we truly are.

It's key to remember that the answers you come up with aren't set in stone. Grief changes, and so will your answers. Whenever these big questions bubble up, take some time to mull them over again. As we finish exploring these big questions that come with grief, it's clear that this isn't just about finding neat and tidy answers. It's more about what we learn along the way, the people we get closer to, and the choices we make. It's learning how to keep living with our loss, keeping our loved ones close, not just in our memories but woven into our day-to-day lives.

As we keep going, let's have the guts to face these questions head-on, be open to where they might take us, and find the strength to hold on to the answers we uncover. Doing this is a way to honor both our loved ones and ourselves as we keep growing, healing, and figuring out new ways to see the world.

Chapter 6: *O*pen a New Chapter

"Life is not the way it is supposed to be. It is the way it is. The way you cope with it is what makes the difference." ~ Virginia Satir

Picture this: you're strolling through your favorite part of town, the one with the quirky shops and that coffee place you love. Out of nowhere, a wave of grief hits you—hard. Maybe it's the sight of a couple holding hands, or perhaps it's a song floating out from a store, one that you and your loved one used to jam out to together. Suddenly, you're not just walking; you're wading through a sea of emotions, trying to keep your head above water. We've all been there, blindsided by grief at the most unexpected times. It's moments like these when having a set of quick coping strategies and an emotional first aid kit can be a lifesaver.

Emotional Triage

Recognizing Emotional Crisis

Sometimes, it's not the significant anniversaries or holidays that trip us up; it's the small, everyday moments that catch us off guard, like realizing you're shopping for one at the store. Knowing the signs of an emotional crisis can help you act swiftly to manage your grief. These signs might include:

- A sudden feeling of overwhelming sadness or anxiety
- Physical symptoms like a racing heart or difficulty breathing
- An urge to isolate yourself from others
- Intrusive thoughts about your loss that you can't seem to shake off

Seeing these signs for what they are—a natural response to your loss—can be the first step toward managing them.

Self-Soothing Techniques

When grief hits like a tidal wave, having some self-soothing techniques at the ready can help you find your footing again. Here are a few strategies that you might find helpful:

- **Deep Breathing**: Simple, yet effective. Try the 4-7-8 technique: breathe in for 4 seconds, hold for 7, and exhale for 8. It's a quick way to calm your nervous system.
- **Grounding Exercises**: These are designed to bring you back to the here and now. A popular one is the 5-4-3-2-1 technique, where you identify 5 things you can see, 4 you can touch, 3 you can hear, 2 you can smell, and 1 you can

taste. It's surprisingly effective at pulling you back from the edge of a grief spiral.

- **Move Your Body**: Sometimes, the best way to shake off that wave of grief is, well, to literally shake it off. If you can, take a quick walk, stretch, or dance around your living room—whatever gets you moving.

Creating an Emotional First Aid Kit

Think of this as your go-to box (or bag or digital playlist) of comfort and coping tools for when grief catches you off guard. Here's what you might include:

- A playlist of songs that boost your spirits or soothe your soul
- A small object or trinket that brings you comfort, like a stone from a favorite beach or a piece of jewelry
- A list of affirmations that remind you of your strength and resilience
- A comforting scent, like a small vial of essential oil or a sachet of lavender
- Photos that bring back happy memories
- A journal or app for quick, on-the-go reflections

Having this kit ready means you're prepared for those unexpected moments of grief, equipped with tools that you know can help ease your pain.

Emergency Contacts

In the thick of a grief wave, remembering who you can turn to for support can be tricky. That's why having a list of emergency contacts is crucial. This list might include:

- A trusted friend or family member who's a good listener
- Your therapist or counselor, if you have one
- Hotlines or text services specifically for emotional support or crisis intervention
- Support groups or online forums where you can share what you're going through

Having these contacts saved on your phone or written down in your emotional first aid kit means you're never alone, even in your most challenging moments. I suggest you also ensure the In Case of Emergency (ICE) contacts are up-to-date and flagged as such in your phone.

Navigating through grief isn't about avoiding the waves but learning how to ride them. With these strategies close by, you're better equipped to face those sudden surges of emotion, knowing you have the tools and support to help you through. It's about giving yourself grace in these moments, recognizing that grief is a part of your story but not the entirety of it. And most importantly, it's about remembering that even in the depths of sorrow, there are lifelines to help pull you back to solid ground.

The Overlooked Effects of Grief and Physical Wellness

When the heart is heavy with grief, it's not just our spirits that feel the weight; our bodies bear the burden, too. It's easy to forget, amidst the emotional turmoil, that grief doesn't just reside in our minds but manifests physically. The ache of a heart missing someone isn't just symbolic; it can translate to tangible pain, fatigue, or a host of other symptoms, as we touched on in Chapter 1. Recognizing this dual impact of grief is the first step toward nurturing both mind and body back to a state of balance.

Physical Health and Grief's Grip

The toll that grief takes on the body might surprise you. You might find your sleep pattern disrupted, your appetite changed, or your energy levels fluctuating wildly. These are not just signs of emotional distress but physical expressions of your grief. Much like the ocean reflects the state of the sky above, our bodies mirror our emotional landscapes. Acknowledging this can empower you to take steps that address both emotional and physical healing as interlinked parts of your grief process.

The Body-Mind Connection

The link between moving our bodies and lifting our spirits is something we've known for a while, and is well-documented, especially when we're walking through the shadows of grief. In those moments, a little bit of movement can be a soft yet strong way to push back against the stillness that sadness often leaves us in. It's not about intense workouts or testing how far we can go, but rather discovering gentle movements that help us feel

104

the rhythm of life again. This is about reconnecting with our bodies, which are going through their own kind of mourning, and finding comfort in that shared journey.

Gentle Exercise

For those dealing with loss, gentle exercise can help ground and focus you. Consider these activities not as tasks to check off but as invitations to reconnect with your body and breathe space into your grieving heart:

- **Walking**: Perhaps the simplest form of movement, it's also the most grounding. Let each step be a moment of connection to the earth, a reminder that you are here, you are moving, you are alive.
- **Yoga**: With its emphasis on breath and mindful movement, yoga can be a sanctuary for those in grief. It allows you to hold space for your sorrow while gently stretching your body and spirit toward healing.
- **Tai Chi**: This martial art, known for its slow, flowing movements, can be a moving meditation, offering balance and peace in moments of turmoil.

Listening to Your Body

Your body speaks its own language and informs you of its needs through fatigue, restlessness, or tension. Learning to listen, to truly hear what it's saying, requires patience and practice. It might tell you to rest when you feel you should be "doing" something or ask for movement when you feel like staying still. Tuning into these messages allows you to respond with kindness, giving your body the care it needs to support you.

Starting Small

Integrating physical wellness into your grief process doesn't have to begin with grand gestures. You don't need to run a marathon or even 5K. Small, manageable activities are the stepping stones that can significantly change how you feel physically and emotionally. Here are a few suggestions:

- **A Stretching Routine**: Begin and end your day with a few gentle stretches. This can help alleviate physical tension and bring a sense of ritual and care to your daily routine.
- **Breathing Exercises**: Integrating simple breathing exercises into your day can help calm your mind and body, making it easier to cope with moments of intense emotion.
- **Nature Walks**: Regular walks in the natural world, with its cycles of growth and renewal, can offer a perspective and peace that can be comforting in times of grief.

Embracing these practices can be a form of self-care, a way to honor both the emotional and physical aspects of your grief. Healing encompasses the whole self, inviting a gentle alignment of body and spirit as you navigate through your loss.

Mindfulness and Grief: Staying Present Amidst Pain

F inding calm in the maelstrom of grief can seem an impossible task. Yet, within this storm, mindfulness can anchor us, offering a place of tranquility and a reminder that a center of calm exists. Mindfulness isn't about silencing the storm but learning to find peace within it.

Grounding Techniques

Imagine you're a tree, your roots digging deep into the earth, stable and secure. This visualization is at the heart of grounding techniques, methods designed to tether you to the present when past memories or future anxieties threaten to sweep you away. Here are a few you might find helpful:

- **Touch**: Keep a small item in your pocket, like a smooth stone or a soft piece of fabric. When overwhelmed, hold it. Concentrate on its texture, temperature, and weight. I had a "worry stone" in my pocket for years.
- **Sight**: Choose an object in your vicinity. Observe it closely, noting its colors, shapes, and any patterns or imperfections. This focus pulls you back to the now.
- **Hearing**: Close your eyes and tune in to the sounds around you. Try to identify as many as possible, from the distant to the near, the rhythmic to the random.

Mindful Awareness

Mindful awareness is about observing your experiences— thoughts, emotions, and physical sensations—without judgment. It's recognizing that grief is a multifaceted experience, filled with ups and downs. And that it's okay to feel all of it. Here's how you can cultivate this awareness:

- **Begin with Breathing**: Focus on your breath. Notice the feeling of air entering and leaving your body and your chest's rise and fall.
- **Acknowledge Your Feelings**: As emotions surface, name them. "This is sadness. This is anger." Acknowledgment without judgment allows these feelings to exist without overwhelming you.
- **Accept the Moment**: Remind yourself that this moment, no matter how painful, is part of your experience. Acceptance doesn't mean resignation; it means giving yourself permission to feel, to grieve, and to heal.

Breathing Exercises

Though we breathe without thought most of the time, breathing exercises are a bridge between body and mind, a simple yet profound tool that can center and calm us. During moments of intense grief, breathing exercises can be a lifeline, drawing us back from the edge of despair. You'll notice we frequently come back to focused breathing as a coping mechanism. Try these additional techniques:

- **Square Breathing**: Visualize drawing a square. Inhale for a count of four as you draw the first side, hold for four as you draw the second, exhale for four along the third, and hold again for four to complete the square. This pattern can help regulate your breathing and focus your mind.
- **Sighing Breath**: Take a deep breath in, filling your lungs completely. Then, open your mouth and let it out in a long, audible sigh. This exercise can release tension and

refresh your mind. Bonus: You may find that the louder you sigh, the better you feel.

Daily Mindfulness Practice

Bringing mindfulness into your daily routine can build a foundation of stability and acceptance to support you. Here's how you might integrate it:

- **Morning Intentions**: Start your day by setting an intention. It could be a word or phrase that embodies how you want to approach the day, like "patience" or "openness."
- **Mindful Eating**: Use meals as an opportunity to practice mindfulness. Eat slowly, savoring each bite, paying attention to the flavors, textures, and the act of nourishing your body. More on this in a moment.
- **Evening Reflection**: End your day with a few minutes of reflection. Consider three moments from the day for which you're grateful or three emotions you experienced, exploring them with curiosity and without judgment.

Through grounding techniques, mindful awareness, and breathing exercises, you cultivate an inner sanctuary, a place of calm within the storm, where healing can begin and where you can find the strength to face each day with an open heart. Mindfulness doesn't require perfection, only presence.

Nourishing Your Grieving Soul: Mindful Eating in Times of Loss

We touched on mindful eating a moment ago as a daily practice to bring into your life. There's a deep connection between what we eat and how we feel physically and emotionally. This link is especially poignant during loss, where nourishing our body can also mean nourishing our soul.

Nutrition and Mood

The food we consume plays a critical role in our overall well-being, affecting not just our physical health but our emotional state as well. Nutrients like omega-3 fatty acids, found in fish and flaxseeds, can boost mood, while antioxidants in fruits and vegetables combat stress. Meanwhile, processed foods and high sugar intake can have the opposite effect, leading to energy crashes and heightened anxiety. Recognizing this connection is the first step toward using mindful eating to support our healing. By choosing foods that fuel our body and mind, we can gently support our journey through grief, making each meal an opportunity for self-care.

Comfort Foods

There's no denying the temporary solace that comfort foods can bring. Whether it's a family recipe that reminds us of happier times or simply a dish that feels like a warm hug, these foods hold a special place in our hearts, especially during periods of mourning. However, balancing these moments of indulgence with our nutritional needs is key. Here are a few tips to strike that balance:

- **Moderation is Key**: Allow yourself to enjoy these foods without guilt, but be mindful of moderation. It's about finding a balance that honors your emotional needs without compromising your physical health.
- **Healthy Twists**: Experiment with adapting your favorite comfort foods to include more nutritious ingredients. This can be a playful way to enjoy the flavors you love while caring for your body.
- **Listen to Your Body**: Pay attention to how certain foods make you feel afterward. If you notice that some items exacerbate feelings of sluggishness or sadness, consider limiting them and see if it improves your overall mood.

Mindful Cooking

Cooking can go beyond its primary function of meal preparation to become a meditative, healing activity. When we cook mindfully, we're fully present with the process—the chopping, the stirring, the sizzling sounds, and the aromatic scents. This mindfulness turns cooking into a form of therapy, grounding us in the here and now. Moreover, preparing dishes our loved ones enjoyed can be a beautiful way to honor their memory, keeping their spirit alive in our kitchens and hearts. Here's how to embrace mindful cooking:

- **Set the Scene**: Before you begin, take a few moments to clear your cooking space and your mind. A tidy kitchen and a focused intention can set the stage for a mindful cooking experience.
- **Engage Your Senses**: As you cook, pay close attention to the textures of the ingredients, the sounds of cooking,

and the aromas that fill the air. This sensory engagement can bring a deep sense of calm and connection.

- **Cook with Love**: Remind yourself that each meal you prepare is an act of self-love, self-care, and a tribute to those you're remembering. This perspective turns the act of cooking into something meaningful.

Shared Meals

Sharing a meal with others has always been a powerful way to connect, offering sanctuary and support without needing words. In times of grief, this communal act can be particularly healing. Whether it's a simple weeknight dinner with family or a potluck with friends where everyone brings a dish that their loved one adored, shared meals create a space for memories to be cherished and for the bonds of support to be strengthened. Here are a few ways to make the most of shared meals:

- **Invite Conversation**: Use mealtime to share stories and memories of your loved one. This can be a comforting way to keep their spirit a part of your gatherings.
- **Create New Traditions**: Consider starting new mealtime traditions that honor your journey through grief. This could be a monthly dinner where everyone shares something they're grateful for.
- **Offer and Accept Help**: If cooking feels too overwhelming, don't hesitate to accept meal offers from friends and family. Likewise, offering to cook for someone else who's grieving can be a beautiful gesture of support.

By bringing mindful eating into our daily lives, we find a path through grief that honors our loved ones and our own healing process. It's a journey that acknowledges the power of nourishment in all its forms—physical, emotional, and communal—guiding us gently toward a place of renewal and strength.

The Power of Routine in Grief Recovery

G rief, by its unpredictable nature, disrupts the rhythm of daily life, turning what was once familiar into something strangely unrecognizable. In the wake of such upheaval, establishing a routine can be a beacon of steadiness, a way to tether ourselves to the semblance of normalcy amidst the chaos of loss. This isn't about adhering to a rigid schedule that leaves no room for the nuances of mourning. Instead, it's about crafting a flexible structure that supports and adapts to our healing process, one step at a time.

Establishing Normalcy

Clinging to or re-establishing daily routines can serve as a lifeline. Whether brewing morning coffee or a nightly skincare regimen, these routines act as familiar markers in an unfamiliar world. They remind us of life's continuity, that, despite everything, the world keeps turning, and so too must we, however slowly. Start by identifying small, manageable parts of your pre-loss routine that you can reintegrate or new ones that bring comfort. The key lies in the familiarity of the tasks, not the complexity, and in the sense of accomplishment and normalcy they can restore.

Simple Tasks Matter

There's something quietly powerful about the small, everyday things we do. Tidying up your bed, caring for your plants, or putting together a simple meal might feel like climbing mountains when your heart is heavy with grief. But believe it or not, these simple acts carry so much more weight than they seem. They remind you of your own strength and resilience. On those days when the sadness feels too much to bear, let these tiny victories whisper, "You've got this. You'll make it through."

You might start by identifying three "non-negotiables" each day. These should be simple, achievable tasks that serve as a bare minimum to help guide your day.

Flexibility is Key

Just as the tides ebb and flow, so does the intensity of grief. I keep coming back to the wave metaphor because it works. Some days, the waters are calm, and navigating your routine feels almost effortless. On other days, the waves crash relentlessly, making even the simplest tasks impossible. On these turbulent days, flexibility is your ally. Allow your routine to ebb and flow with your needs, understanding that scaling back is okay. This flexibility transforms your routine from a rigid structure to a supportive framework that bends but does not break under grief's unpredictable weight.

- **Adapt as Needed**: If your planned tasks feel too daunting, scale them down. A walk around the block can become a few minutes of fresh air on your doorstep.
- **Listen to Your Heart**: Some days, what you need may not be on your to-do list. Be open to adjusting your plans, prioritizing what feels most healing.

I remember when I first started consulting, after my first loss, I traveled across the country to orientation and was greeted by one of the VPs during his welcome speech. He held up a green Gumby doll and said, "This is what you need to be. You need to be flexible to be successful." I remember the speech and sentiment, not the executive who gave it.

Sleep and Grief: Restoring Your Mind and Body

In the grip of grief, sleep can feel like a distant dream. Our thoughts spin, restless with loss, making true rest elusive. Yet, in those quiet hours of sleep, we find a haven for healing. Recognizing what keeps us awake is the first gentle step toward inviting sleep back in, allowing us to rest and heal.

Sleep Disruptions

When you're grieving, nights can feel endlessly long. Maybe you wake up a lot, have trouble falling asleep, or dreams and nightmares keep you from feeling rested. These aren't just minor annoyances; they really can throw off your whole day, messing with your mood, focus, and health. Knowing these sleep troubles come from your grief is the first step toward handling them with care and finding ways to cope.

Bedtime Rituals

Creating rituals to signal to your body and mind that it's time to wind down can be extremely effective. Consider adding one or more of these practices into your nightly routine:

- **Warm Baths**: The soothing warmth of a bath can help relax both your body and mind. Add in some lavender oil for its calming properties.
- **Reading**: Immersing yourself in a book allows you to step outside your thoughts for a while, making it easier to drift off to sleep.
- **Gentle Yoga or Stretching**: Simple stretches can release the physical tension that accumulates during the day, signaling to your body that it's time to rest.

- **Meditation or Guided Imagery**: Listening to a guided meditation or visualization can distract your thoughts and ease you into sleep.

Creating a ritual that resonates with you can transform your approach to bedtime, making it a time of solace rather than struggle.

Comforting Environment
The space where you sleep plays a crucial role in how well you rest. A few adjustments can make a world of difference:

- **Keep It Cool and Dark**: A cooler, darker environment is more conducive to sleep. Consider blackout curtains and adjust your thermostat to find a temperature that's comfortable for you.
- **Limit Screen Time**: The blue light from screens can interfere with your body's natural sleep cycles. Try to disconnect at least an hour before bed.
- **Surround Yourself with Comfort**: Ensure your bedding is comfortable and inviting. Adding a few extra pillows or a weighted blanket can create a sense of security and comfort.

Tailoring your sleeping space to meet your needs can help create an oasis of calm, inviting the restorative sleep you need.

Professional Help
If sleep still dodges you, no matter how hard you try, it might be a signal to get some expert advice. Ignoring ongoing sleep issues isn't good for your body or mind, and asking for help is perfectly okay. Sleep experts or therapists can guide you with

personalized advice and support. They often recommend cognitive behavioral therapy for insomnia (CBT-I), a proven method that tackles the thoughts and habits affecting your sleep. Remember, seeking help shows courage and a commitment to your healing journey.

In those late hours, when sleep feels just beyond grasp, know you're not walking this path alone. Small changes in your daily habits and your surroundings and possibly seeking professional support can pave the way for the restful nights you deserve. In these peaceful slumbers, healing begins to bloom, empowering you to face each new day with fresh energy and clarity.

Putting the Pieces Back Together

After losing someone close, it's like you're in the middle of what used to be your life, surrounded by pieces of a world you once shared. Starting over might feel overwhelming, like trying to solve a puzzle when the pieces just don't match up anymore. But there's a silver lining in this challenge – it's a chance to find out who you are now, in this new world without them. It's about picking up those pieces, one by one, and building something that pays tribute to what you've lost and looks forward to what's ahead.

Finding Yourself Again

The person you are after loss is not the same person you were before. Though it may sting, this truth is not a sentence to a diminished life but an invitation to growth. In the act of putting the pieces back together, you can discover new facets of yourself, strengths you didn't know you possessed, and passions that had lain dormant. This is where I rediscovered my love for acting.

- **Reflect on Your Values**: Your core values might shift after experiencing loss. Take time to reflect on what matters most to you now. This could involve writing down your values and considering how they align with your life as it is today.
- **Explore New Interests**: It's common for interests to evolve as you navigate grief. Allow yourself the freedom to explore new hobbies or activities. This exploration can be a path to discovering new joys and passions.
- **Embrace Change**: Accept that change is inevitable in life and growth. Embracing this change can open doors to

119

new opportunities and ways of living that bring fulfillment and happiness.

Self-Care: Loving the Living

Remembering to love yourself and care for the person who has survived and *is* surviving is paramount. Your existence and your well-being still hold immense value, and nurturing yourself is not selfishness; it's an act of survival and reverence for the life you continue to live.

- **The Importance of Self-Care**: Caring for yourself is a way to honor your resilience and your journey. It's an acknowledgment that your well-being matters, profoundly affecting your ability to navigate grief and embrace life.
- **Beginning a Self-Care Practice**: Start small. Self-care doesn't have to be grand gestures; it can be as simple as ensuring you're hydrated, taking a few minutes daily to breathe deeply, or stepping outside to feel the sun on your face.
- **Ideas to Add to Your Routine**:
    - **Physical Self-Care**: Engage in regular, gentle exercise. Prioritize restful sleep. Nourish your body with foods that make you feel good. Consider yoga or tai chi, which harmonize physical movement with breathing. Regular walks, especially in green spaces, can uplift your physical health.
    - **Emotional Self-Care**: Allow yourself time to process your emotions. Journaling can be a powerful tool for this. Seek supportive companionship, whether from friends, family, or

support groups. Creative expression through art, music, or writing can be an emotional release. Connecting with others who understand your loss can provide emotional sustenance.

- **Spiritual Self-Care**: This can include meditation, spending time in nature, or engaging in any practice that connects you to a sense of peace and purpose. Remember, spirituality is personal and doesn't have to align with religious traditions to be meaningful. Practices like mindfulness or gratitude journaling can foster a spiritual connection to the present moment, helping you find peace and acceptance in the now.

Nature's Embrace: The Healing Power of the Outdoors

I n the solitude of nature, with its unspoken rhythms and cycles, a profound source of healing exists. With its resilience and beauty, the natural world mirrors the journey of grief and recovery, reminding us that growth and renewal are ever-present forces in our lives. Engaging with nature can be both a refuge and a teacher, offering lessons in patience, resilience, and the transformative power of time.

- **Nature's Therapeutic Effects**: Studies have shown that time spent in nature can significantly reduce symptoms of anxiety, depression, and stress. It's as though the natural world absorbs some of our pain, replacing it with a sense of calm and connectedness.
- **Simple Outdoor Activities**: The beauty of nature is that it asks for nothing but our presence. Simple activities like walking through a park, sitting by a body of water, or gardening can be incredibly therapeutic. These moments offer a pause, a breath of fresh air in the literal and metaphorical sense.
- **Solitude vs. Social Outings**: Alone, nature offers a space for reflection and connection with oneself. With others, it provides a shared experience that can strengthen bonds with others, offering mutual support without needing words.
- **Memorial Gardens**: Creating a garden in memory of a loved one can be a profoundly healing project. It's a living tribute, a space where memories can bloom alongside your chosen flowers and plants. With its sowing, tending, and harvesting cycles, gardening is a

metaphor for the grief journey, embodying the principles of care, growth, and renewal.

In the embrace of nature, we find a space where grief can exist without confines, where the beauty of life is reflected in the natural world's resilience. Here, in the quiet company of trees, the steady whisper of the wind, and the soft murmur of flowing water, we can find solace, healing, and, perhaps, a renewed sense of connection to the world around us.

Reflecting on Your PURPOSE Journal

We've spent a lot of time in this section because it's all about taking care of yourself so you can experience life while living with grief. I mentioned earlier about the pre-flight announcements that you should "put your mask on before helping others." As a parent flying with my children, those instructions felt counterintuitive, but if I passed out because I didn't put my mask on, I couldn't help my kids. It's the same on the ground: until you take care of yourself, you can't take care of anyone else.

When working on your PURPOSE Journal, remember your prompts for **Open a New Chapter**: What is one small step you can take tomorrow to move forward or do something different? This could be as simple as taking a new route on your walk, trying out a new hobby, doing a self-care ritual, or setting a small, achievable goal.

Reflect upon what you've learned in this chapter and your feelings. Grab a pen and your journal or a piece of paper, and find a comfortable, serene spot where you can be uninterrupted. Take a moment to breathe deeply, centering yourself, and preparing your heart and mind for this journey inward. We're going to spend some time just focusing on your self-care. Again, this isn't a one-and-done exercise. As you read this book, you may not be ready to think of answers to these questions, and that's okay. Think about it as "yet" and return when ready.

- What does "opening a new chapter" mean to you right now? Describe what this new chapter looks like in detail.

- Consider the role of new relationships or strengthening existing ones in your healing journey. What's one step you can take to open yourself to new connections?
- Reflect on the changes you've experienced since your loss. Which change do you find most challenging, and what's one step you can take to adapt more comfortably to it?
- Identify something you've been holding onto that may be hindering your progress. What is it, and how can you begin to let it go?
- What have you discovered about yourself as you consider opening a new chapter? How does this self-awareness contribute to your healing and growth?

Chapter 7: *S*ave Cherished Memories

"Death ends a life, not a relationship. All the love you created is still there. All the memories are still there. You live on—in the hearts of everyone you have touched and nurtured while you were here." ~ Morrie Schwartz

Imagine for a moment a family quilt. Each thread and panel represents a connection, a memory, a shared laugh, or a tear shed in silence. When someone we love passes on, it doesn't mean the end of adding components to this intricate work of art. Instead, we find new colors, textures, and patterns to weave into the fabric of our relationship with them. This chapter is about keeping the threads moving, finding ways to continue the conversation, and embracing the evolving nature of how we relate to those no longer physically with us.

How We Stay Connected

Love Never Dies
Love's resilience is unmatched. It continues to live beyond the physical boundaries of presence and absence, thriving in memory, tradition, and reminders of a shared joke or a favorite song. We keep the love alive for someone who has passed by giving it new expressions.

Love's legacy is how we let it shape our lives. It's in how we allow it to guide us in becoming more compassionate, more understanding, and more connected to the human experience.

Evolving Relationships
Our relationships with those who have passed aren't over; they've evolved into something else. They grow and change as we do, adapting to the changes in our lives. In addition to just remembering our loved ones, we can find active ways to keep these relationships, such as:

- **Letter Writing**: Sometimes, the things we wish we could say pile up. Writing letters to your loved one can be a therapeutic way to keep the dialogue open. You might choose a special notebook for this purpose, making it a tangible representation of your continuing bond. I found writing letters to be helpful in my journey.
- **Reflection Walks**: Take walks in places that hold some special meaning to you. Use this time to reflect on how your bond has evolved, how it influences your choices, and how you carry their spirit with you daily.

New Traditions

Creating new traditions is a way to integrate the memory and essence of your loved one into your current life. It's about finding balance—honoring the past while making space for the future.

- **Memory Jar**: Fill a jar with notes of moments you wish you could share with them, funny things that happened, or ways you saw their influence in your life throughout the year. On a particular day, go through these notes, celebrating their ongoing presence in your life.

Love's Legacy

The love we share shapes us and becomes a part of our own legacy. I know I wouldn't be the same person I am now had it not been for the relationships in my life. The love we share influences how we love others, how we grieve, and how we grow.

- **Acts of Kindness**: Carry out acts of kindness in their memory, such as a candle on a holiday tree or a donation in their memory. What might they have appreciated? This keeps their spirit alive and spreads the love they embodied.

Spiritual Connections

Our spiritual beliefs and practices can offer profound ways to maintain connections with those who have passed. Whether through prayer, meditation, or other rituals, these practices can provide comfort and a sense of closeness.

- **Meditation Space**: Creating a dedicated space in your home for meditation or prayer can be a physical reminder of your connection. Adorn this space with photos, candles, or any item that feels significant.
- **Nature Offerings**: For those who feel a deep connection to the natural world, consider making offerings in nature—planting a tree, for example, or leaving biodegradable tokens of love by the sea.

Remembering those we've lost is not just about looking back; it's about finding ways to carry their essence forward with us. It's in the meals we cook, the songs we play, the letters we write, and the new traditions we forge. It's in the quiet moments of reflection and the acts of kindness done in their name. Our relationships with our departed loved ones continue to evolve, adding new threads and panels to the quilted patchwork of our lives, woven with love, memory, and the unbreakable bonds that transcend absence.

Legacy Projects: Keeping Their Memory Alive

For us, the loss of a loved one stops time; it's as if the world is at a standstill, yet, somehow, … time relentlessly marches on. In the heart of all this, creating a legacy project becomes a beautiful way to keep the memory of our loved ones burning bright. They help turn our sorrow into meaningful actions that reflect their lasting mark on the world. It's like bringing the essence of those we've missed into the very fabric of our community.

Personal Significance

Selecting the right legacy project requires a heart-to-heart conversation with oneself, reflecting on what truly captures the spirit of our loved ones. This process is deeply personal and might need time to align with the essence of who they were and what they stood for. Here's how to approach this:

- **Reflect on Their Passions**: What lit up their eyes? Was it education, nature, art, or community service? Let their passions guide your focus.
- **Consider Their Impact**: Think about how they influenced those around them. Did they have a green thumb, a generous heart, or a knack for inspiring young minds? Choose a project that mirrors this impact.
- **Align with Your Capacity**: Ensure the project is something you can realistically manage or organize, whether on your own or with the support of others.

Collaborative Efforts

The great thing about launching a legacy project is that you don't have to do it alone. In fact, collaboration can amplify its impact, bringing the community together and fostering a collective healing process. Here are a few thoughts on how to engage others in this journey:

- **Family and Friends**: Involve those who also cherish your loved one. This will distribute the workload and enrich the project with diverse perspectives and memories.
- **Community Partnerships**: Contact local organizations, schools, or businesses that might align with your project's goals. Their support can lend credibility, resources, and broader community engagement.
- **Crowdfunding**: For projects requiring substantial funding, crowdfunding platforms can rally local and global communities around your cause, highlighting the far-reaching impact of your loved one's legacy.

Memory Preservation, Impact, and Legacy

Crafting a legacy project requires thought, care, and creativity. The scope of such projects is as vast as the night sky, ranging from scholarships in their name to foundations supporting causes they were passionate about to community gardens that serve as living memorials. Each option shines a light on their values and our love for them. Consider these ideas and how they may work for your project:

- **Scholarships**: Establishing a scholarship fund in your loved one's name provides educational opportunities for others and immortalizes the value of education (or sports, theater, etc.) your loved one advocated.

- **Foundations**: Creating a foundation can amplify their impact on causes close to their hearts, such as environmental conservation, animal welfare, or supporting the arts.
- **Community Projects**: Initiatives like building a playground, renovating a community center, or starting a public library can transform communal spaces, embedding your loved one's legacy into the everyday lives of your community. My second husband was a huge supporter of the schools and was there frequently volunteering; it's as if he needed his own parking spot. After he died, I noticed an article in the local paper about Buddy Benches. Buddy Benches, for those unfamiliar, are intended for children to sit on when they're feeling lonely or looking for someone to play with. Other children see this and choose to be a buddy. I decided to donate one to our Primary School in his memory. I've used his memory to raise funds for the Boys and Girls Club and the Parent Teacher Organization. These were causes he was passionate about in life.

When working on a legacy project, we're doing more than keeping our loved ones' memories alive; we're offering them a seat at the table of the future, ensuring their influence remains a vibrant part of our world. These projects channel our loved ones' passions into the lives of others, impacting those they may have never met. Through thoughtful planning, collaboration, and connecting with who they were, we can craft legacies that honor our loved ones and sow seeds of change, beauty, and hope in the garden of humanity.

Revisiting the Past… Without Staying

O ur past influences our present: we share each memory, moment, and piece of a heart. The challenge isn't in looking back—that's easy. The challenge is in doing so without losing ourselves in what was. It's about holding the past gently in our hands, acknowledging its beauty and its pain while keeping our feet firmly planted in the now. We can't change what happened, and this is part of acceptance.

Keeping Memories Alive

We've shared some public ways to keep memories alive, but we also want to keep those memories alive within. Keeping these memories vibrant should enrich our lives without casting a shadow over the present. We've all got photo albums or boxes of photos; we have odd scraps lying about that remind us of loved ones. Here are a few ideas on what you can do with those:

- **Photo Albums Reimagined**: Transfer old photos to digital formats. Create a slideshow set to music that brings those moments to life, allowing you to revisit them without the heaviness of dust-covered albums.
- **Memory Capsules**: Place mementos—ticket stubs, small notes, a pressed flower—into clear, ornament-sized capsules. Hang these in spaces where light touches, a visual reminder of joy without the weight of a shrine.

Staying Present

The art of staying present, particularly when the past holds so much of who we are and whom we've lost, is much like learning to dance in a storm—acknowledging the rain but focusing on the steps, the music, and the dance itself. We've talked about some of these in terms of mindfulness, but let's review. I don't know about you, but reminders are helpful to me.

- **Mindful Breathing**: Use your breath as an anchor to the present. When memories surge, focus on the rhythm of your breath—inhale the now, exhale the past.
- **Sensory Anchors**: Engage your senses to ground yourself in the moment. A particular scent, the feel of fabric, the taste of mint—simple sensory experiences can tether you to the now, making it easier to visit the past without staying there.
- **Gratitude Glimpses**: Start or end your day by identifying one thing you're grateful for in your present. It could be as simple as a cup of coffee or a moment of silence. This practice shifts focus to the small wonders of the now.

Surviving the Difficult Days

Certain days magnify loss, turning the calendar into a minefield of memories. Among the pieces of advice from *Life After* Losses, I find dealing with triggers and the calendar to be among the most powerful tools at our disposal. Facing difficult days requires foresight and a plan that honors your need to remember while safeguarding your well-being.

- **Pre-plan Your Day**: Decide in advance how you'll spend these difficult days. Whether visiting a special spot, spending time with friends, allowing yourself a day of quiet reflection, or burying your head under the covers, having a plan can provide a sense of control. There's no right or wrong way to do this.

- **Emotional Intentions**: Set an intention for how you wish to feel or what you want to achieve by the end of the day. It could be a sense of peace, a moment of joy, or a connection with their memory that feels more sweet than bitter.
- **Memory Triggers**: Prepare for potential memory triggers. If certain places, songs, or activities are likely to evoke strong emotions, decide in advance how you'll handle them. It might mean changing your route, creating a new playlist, or even starting new traditions that redefine the day.

When we learn to integrate these strategies into our lives, we learn to honor the past and those we've lost without letting them anchor us away from the present. It's a delicate balance of looking back and moving forward while living in the present.

Reflecting on Your PURPOSE Journal

When working on your PURPOSE Journal, remember your prompts for **Save Cherished Memories**: What is a happy memory you have of the person, place, or situation you've lost? How did this memory make you feel today, and what does it remind you of about the relationship or connection? How have you kept the memory alive?

Reflect upon what you've learned in this chapter and your feelings. Grab a pen and your journal or a piece of paper and find a comfortable, serene spot where you can be uninterrupted. Take a moment to breathe deeply, center yourself, and prepare your heart and mind for this journey inward. We're going to spend some time focused on honoring your memories.

- **Evolving Conversation:** If you could have a conversation with your loved one today, what would you want to tell them about your life now? What do you imagine they would say in response? Advanced option: write a conversation between you and your loved one. Focus on "hearing" their voice. I did this many times, and on one occasion, I felt I was actually having a conversation with him.
- **Letters to the Future:** Write a letter to your future self from your loved one's perspective. What words of love, encouragement, or advice do they offer?
- **Acts of Kindness:** Did you perform any act of kindness in memory of your loved one? What did you feel while planning or performing this act?

- **Dream Visit:** Have you ever dreamed about your loved one? Describe the dream and the feelings it evoked. What message or comfort did the dream bring?
- **Gifts of Guidance:** Reflect on a piece of advice or wisdom your loved one gave you. How have you used or lived by that advice in your life?

As we close this chapter, let's remember to cherish our memories of the past, but remain firmly rooted in the present. For those of us who have been widowed, the promise "till death do us part" didn't stop the loving; it simply changed how we love. And as we turn the page, let's carry with us the lessons learned, the love shared, and the gratitude that binds them together, stepping into the next chapter of our lives with open hearts and a renewed sense of hope as we embrace our personal growth.

Chapter 8: *E*mbrace Personal Growth

"You can clutch the past so tightly to your chest that it leaves your arms too full to embrace the present."~ Jan Glidewell

Picture this: you're redecorating your living room. You're rearranging your home's furniture, a mundane yet strangely cathartic task. Each piece shifted brings a new perspective to the room, altering how you interact with the space. It's refreshing, sometimes challenging, but ultimately, it redefines the room's purpose and your comfort within it. This act mirrors the process of rediscovering oneself after a significant loss. It's about shifting, rearranging, and, sometimes, letting go of pieces that no longer fit, all in the pursuit of finding new comfort and purpose in the transformed space of your existence.

A loss can feel like it erases parts of our identity. The roles we played, the future we envisioned, and the daily interactions that defined us suddenly seem to belong to a life that's no longer ours. The task, then, is to sift through the rubble, to find ourselves amidst the remnants, and to piece together a version of self that honors who we were and who we can become. And, yes... I know it's daunting, but it's also vital.

Redefining Identity: Who Am I After Loss?

Personal Reflection

Reflecting on who we are after loss is like standing in front of a mirror, not recognizing the person staring back. It's okay. It's normal. Start with questions that ground you: What values still resonate with me? What activities bring me peace or joy? How do I see my relationship with my loved one now? Reflection is the first step toward clarity. Harken back to Chapter 2 and Perceive Reality. Let's reflect:

- **Reflect on Moments of Fulfillment**: Think back to moments in your life when you felt most fulfilled or at peace. What were you doing? Who were you with? Answers to these questions can highlight values that may have been overshadowed by grief.
- **Consider Your Legacy**: Contemplate what you want your legacy to be. How do you want to be remembered by your friends, family, and community? This exercise can help clarify the values you wish to live by moving forward.

Identity Shifts

Identity shifts are inevitable and have been occurring throughout your life. However, after a loss, these shifts are forced on us, and we don't really have an option but to accept. We're not moving away from who we were or the love we hold for those we've lost. Instead, these shifts in identity highlight growth, adaptation, and resilience. Losing a spouse might mean transitioning from being a partner to finding comfort and strength in solitude or new companionships. Losing a job may shift your identity from a career-driven individual to someone who finds meaning in volunteer work or creative pursuits. Redefining who we are and who we perceive ourselves to be is something we've done our entire lives; child, student, husband, brother, widower, etc. Most of the time, these redefinitions are subtle based on choices we've made; other times, they are thrust upon us without warning.

Embracing the New Self

Embracing the new version of oneself is perhaps the most challenging step. It involves metaphorically looking at your reflection, with all its changes and new facets, and accepting it with kindness. Start small. Maybe it's adopting a new hobby that your former self hadn't considered or allowing yourself to explore new beliefs and philosophies. It could be as simple as changing your routine. For myself, it was looking back at my life, and it became about sharing my story and stories that matter to me. So, I started writing and then took up acting again after 30+ years.

Continuing Bonds

Maintaining a bond with the one you lost also reshapes your identity. It's not about clinging to what was but finding ways to integrate their memory and essence into your evolving self, as we discussed earlier. Plant a garden of their favorite flowers so every bloom reminds you of them. Start a project they were passionate about and carry it forward in their honor. These acts keep their spirit alive within you and help you in redefining who you are.

The journey of rediscovery after loss is full of introspection and acceptance. It includes folding your memories into your new identity (and if you just flashed on a scene from *Schitt's Creek*, we could be friends). It's about finding balance, embracing change, and allowing the love we carry for those we've lost to help guide us forward. I know it sounds daunting, but the good news is that you've spent a lifetime changing your identity, likely without realizing it. Who you are now is shaped by your life experiences, and you are not the same person you used to be. Embrace the growth.

Setting New Goals: The Path to Rediscovery

When the Earth quakes, and our world tilts on its axis, we're left with our footing on unfamiliar ground. This terrain looks scary, but , strangely, it also gives us a new opportunity to assess the direction we want to take our lives, and gives us the opportunity to chart a course that aligns with our new reality. It's like standing at a crossroads, map in hand, deciding which path to take—not just to move forward but to rediscover who we are and what we cherish most in this altered landscape. And just because we take a few steps in one direction doesn't mean we're stuck with that choice forever. We get to (remember that language?) alter paths as needed until we feel fulfilled.

Goal Adjustment

Adjusting our goals isn't about giving up your dreams. It's simply acknowledging that life has changed, and so must our aims. My goal to retire with my husband ended with his life. For a long time, I couldn't dream again. I have a friend who makes a living by reminding us, "Life gets in the way." We learn to adjust as a result, and this adjustment isn't a step back but a recalibration. We get to (there I go again) ensure our goals resonate with who we are becoming in the aftershocks of our loss. It's about asking, "What matters to me now?" and allowing the answer to guide our new objectives.

- Start by listing existing goals, then honestly evaluate which still hold meaning. It's okay to let go of those that no longer fit.
- Make new goals that reflect your current values and circumstances. This might mean prioritizing personal

well-being, seeking connections, or pursuing previously
sidelined passions.

Small Steps

The prospect of setting and achieving goals after a loss can feel
overwhelming. The key is to break them down into small,
manageable steps. Doing so transforms a large goal into a series
of achievable actions, each as a building block to something
greater.

- Break each goal into smaller tasks, ensuring each is clear
  and actionable.
- Remember to celebrate completing these tasks, no matter
  how minor they seem. This reinforces a sense of
  accomplishment and propels you forward.

Finding Meaning

After a loss, goals become reflections of our journey. They
become signposts on our healing path and monuments to what
we've endured and overcome. Finding meaning in new goals
involves connecting them to the larger story of our lives,
making sure they contribute to a sense of purpose and
fulfillment.

- Infuse your goals with personal significance. If a loved
  one inspired a love for nature, consider goals that honor
  that connection, such as conservation efforts or outdoor
  adventures.
- Align goals with your values. If family has become a
  central pillar, set goals that enhance these relationships,
  fostering quality time and shared experiences.

Celebrating Progress

On the path toward recovery, every step forward deserves recognition. We've talked about celebrating even the smallest win. Celebrating progress isn't just about acknowledging achievements; it's a vital part of the healing process. It reminds us of our strength, resilience, and capacity to grow despite adversity.

- Create a ritual for celebrating progress. This might be as simple as literally patting yourself on the back or a quiet moment of gratitude.
- Share your achievements with others. This allows you to celebrate together and reinforces your support network, a crucial component of navigating grief. I remember when Sally, a member of my bereavement support group, came in one night excited. "I just bought my first car!" Her husband used to negotiate car prices, and Sally found growth and confidence by doing it herself.

In this section on setting new goals, we've explored some ways to recalibrate our goals and (dare I say it?) dreams to match our transformed selves. We break overwhelming objectives into manageable actions, find the personal significance of those goals, and recognize every step of progress along this path. Through this approach, we navigate our grief and also begin to define our new reality.

Volunteering: Healing through Helping Others

One of the things I suggest people who are grieving do when they don't know where to direct the love they still have for their loved one is to take a path not many consider at first. This path isn't designed with the intention of escaping grief; instead, it's lined with the potential for healing through giving. Volunteering is a bridge that connects us to the world beyond our sorrow. It puts the power of altruism in the light and has the ability to mend the heart. I found, many times, my loss was put in perspective.

Altruism's Benefits

When we step out of our inner turmoil to lend a hand to someone in need, a subtle yet significant shift occurs within us. Altruism, the selfless concern for the well-being of others, lights up parts of our brain associated with pleasure, social connection, and trust. In helping others, we activate a part of ourselves that insists on finding hope. The benefits are multifaceted:

- A decrease in feelings of loneliness and isolation as we connect with those we help.
- An increase in our sense of purpose, reminding us that we have the power to make a difference.
- A reduction in the intensity of our grief symptoms, as focusing on others can provide temporary relief from our pain.

Finding the Right Cause

Choosing where to dedicate your time and energy is a deeply personal decision and can also be a beautiful tribute to your loved one. Here's how you can find a cause that resonates with you and honors your loved one's memory, which you'll find reminiscent as we talked of legacy projects:

- Reflect on their passions and interests. Was there a cause or charity they were particularly fond of? Directing your efforts here can feel like continuing their legacy.
- Consider causes that address the circumstances of your loss. For example, if your loved one battled a long illness, volunteering at a health foundation can feel like a meaningful way to contribute.
- Look for opportunities that align with your skills and interests. Volunteering should also be fulfilling, offering an outlet for your talents and passions.

Community Connection

One of the hidden treasures of volunteering is the community it introduces us to. By volunteering, I became a part of several communities, and have made life-long friendships with like-minded people in the process. These connections are built on shared goals and compassion, creating a sense of belonging. It was exactly what this grieving individual yearned for. Here's what stands out:

- The volunteer community often understands the value of support and empathy, making it a safe space to share your story when ready.

- Working toward a common goal fosters a unique bond that can lead to lasting friendships and a support network.
- Participating in group activities or events reduces the feeling of isolation, reminding you that you're not alone in your desire to make a positive impact.

Personal Growth

Volunteering provides us with growth and self-discovery opportunities. It's not uncommon for individuals to feel transformed by their experiences volunteering. They gain insights and strengths they weren't aware of. Here are some ways this unfolds:

- Facing new challenges and stepping out of your comfort zone can feel scary, but it can also bolster your confidence and resilience.
- Giving can shift your perspective, helping you see your situation in a new light and appreciate the moments of joy and gratitude that exist despite your grief.
- Engaging in charitable acts can fire up a passion for causes you weren't previously connected to, leading to new personal and professional growth paths.

Volunteering can be a salve for the soul when we're suffering. It reminds us that even in our darkest times, we can bring light to others, which, in turn, reflects back on us, perhaps leading us toward healing, connection, and finding a renewed purpose.

Learning from Loss: Grief as a Teacher

In the quiet spaces left behind by those we've lost, there lies
an unexpected teacher: grief itself. Surprisingly, we uncover
truths about the world and ourselves that reshape our
understanding and approach to life. I've called it "life lessons
through grief." The biggest, most important lessons I've learned
in my life have come in the aftermath of a storm. The quiet time
for reflection invites us to listen, learn, and grow.

Life Lessons

From the moment loss touches our lives, the world shifts,
introducing us to lessons we might never have encountered
otherwise. These aren't lessons one finds in textbooks. They're
the insights that come from experiencing love, loss, and the
intricate dance between them. Here are a few:

- The impermanence of life becomes more than a concept;
  it's a reality that teaches us to cherish each moment and
  the people we share them with. This is where my title,
  Life After Losses, comes from.
- We learn about the strength and importance of
  connections and how relationships can exist beyond
  physical presence, continuing to influence us.
- We understand that authentic connections and healing
  occur when we take the risky step of opening our hearts
  and being vulnerable.

Resilience Building

Walking through the valley of grief, we discover resilience, not as a trait we're born with, but as a muscle we build through facing adversity. This resilience encompasses our ability to:

- Know that even the most intense feelings of sadness or anger will ebb, leaving us more equipped to handle future challenges.
- Find light in the darkest times, an ability that shows others there's a path to navigating their sorrow.
- Adapt to new realities, understanding that change, though painful, can lead to new beginnings and opportunities for growth.

Empathy Expansion

Loss softens us, opening our hearts to the suffering of others in a way we might not have thought of. I refer to it as wearing my heart on my sleeve. This expanded empathy allows us to:

- Connect more deeply with those around us, recognizing the shared human experience of pain, love, and loss.
- Offer support rooted in genuine understanding and compassion, becoming a source of comfort for others in their times of need.
- Approach the world with a kinder, more compassionate lens, seeing beyond the surface, down to each person's struggles.

New Perspectives

Grief also alters our perspectives. It shifts how we view life, relationships, and even ourselves going forward. These new viewpoints encourage us to:

- Re-evaluate what truly matters, which usually leads to a reprioritization of time, energy, and resources toward what brings genuine fulfillment.
- Embrace the complexity of emotions, understanding that joy and sorrow can coexist and that acknowledging each enriches our lives.
- Deepen our connections, recognizing the preciousness of those we love and the importance of expressing that love while we can.

When grief becomes a teacher, we're invited to sit at its feet and learn. These lessons borne from pain carry the potential to transform us; they can guide us toward a life marked by greater resilience, empathy, and a deeper appreciation for life and the human experience if we're willing to listen. Through this learning, we honor those we've lost and prepare ourselves to move forward with a heart more open to love, a spirit more resilient to change, and a mind more focused on the beauty of the present moment.

Finding Your Voice: Advocacy and Sharing Your Story

There is a unique narrative in our stories, written by our unique love, loss, and resilience. When we dare to share these stories, we do more than recount what happened; we extend a hand to those walking a similar path in solidarity for the shared human experience that binds us all. This act of sharing isn't just cathartic for the storyteller; it's a beacon of hope for the listener, a reminder that they're not alone in their journey through sorrow. When I wrote *Life After Losses*, it was built upon a book I'd penned nearly a quarter-century earlier. Back then, I thought my story needed to be told, but I was young and lacked the perspective of life and the second loss. It's precisely because of that second loss that I felt my story had meaning. That became my calling: to share my story to inspire others because if I could get through being widowed twice before I turned 48, anyone could survive loss and learn to live life again.

Storytelling Power

The act of sharing our grief journey does more than document our experiences; it transforms them. It allows us to process our emotions, to find meaning in the chaos, and to recognize our growth amidst the pain. I mentioned earlier that I found gratitude for my journey when telling my story in *Life After Losses*. More importantly, sharing our story creates a space for connection, empathy, and understanding. When we do so, we invite others into our world; we offer them a glimpse of the strength and vulnerability that come with loss.

This sharing can take many forms, and each platform offers a unique way to reach out, to touch the lives of others with our words, and to find comfort in the knowledge that our experiences might light the way and inspire someone else.

Advocacy Work

For many, the experience of loss ignites a passion for advocacy, turning personal tragedy into a force for change. This work can be as varied as the stories that inspire it, driven by the desire to honor our loved ones and to make a difference in the lives of others. Here's how personal loss can fuel advocacy efforts:

- Establishing or supporting charities and foundations that align with causes your loved one was passionate about or that address the circumstances of your loss.
- Lobbying for policy changes that improve support systems for the bereaved, whether in healthcare, workplace rights, or public awareness campaigns.
- Volunteering with organizations that aid others in navigating their grief, using your experience to offer guidance, support, and understanding.

In stepping into the role of advocate, we channel our grief, and sometimes our anger in grief, into action, creating a legacy of love and change that transcends our loss.

Platforms for Sharing

In today's digital age, the avenues for sharing our stories are vast and varied, each offering a different way to connect with others. Here are a few platforms to consider:

- **Blogs and Personal Websites**: Ideal for longer, more reflective narratives, blogs offer the space to delve deep into one's journey and explore the nuances of grief and healing.
- **Social Media**: Platforms like Instagram, Facebook, and X (formerly Twitter) allow for more immediate, bite-sized sharing, reaching a broad audience with posts, photos, and short stories.
- **Podcasts and YouTube Channels**: For those comfortable speaking rather than writing, these platforms offer a way to share their story through voice and video, adding a personal touch to their narrative.
- **Speaking Engagements**: Whether at conferences, workshops, or community events, speaking engagements offer a powerful way to connect with an audience, sharing your story and the lessons learned with a live audience.

Each platform offers its own set of strengths, allowing you to choose the one that best suits your style, story, and audience.

Inspiring Others

Sharing our grief journey isn't just about personal expression; it's also about lighting a path for others—setting those luminarias up along the path. It offers hope amid despair, guidance amidst confusion, and understanding within isolation. Here's the impact your story can have:

- **Empowering Others**: Hearing how someone has navigated their grief can empower others to face their own, providing them with strategies, insights, and the knowledge that recovery is possible.

- **Building Community**: Shared stories are the foundation of community, creating bonds of understanding and empathy to support and sustain those in grief.
- **Promoting Healing**: Both the act of sharing and the act of listening can be profoundly healing, offering the storyteller and the audience a way to process their emotions and find solace in shared experiences.

In the end, finding your voice and sharing your story is a journey of personal healing. But it's also a gift to others and a ripple of change in the vast ocean of grief. It's a testament to our abilities as humans to be strong and resilient and our capacity to let love continue to guide us, even in the absence of those we've lost.

The Power of Hope: Looking to the Future

E ventually, the intensity of our grief subsides, offering a glimmer that hope can emerge among the remnants. This delicate power guides us toward brighter days, inspiring us to imagine a future where the ache of loss becomes a part of us yet does not define us, where we can live with the grief and not for it. Grief doesn't confine us; it proves our ability to love deeply, grow, and begin anew.

Cultivating Hope

Nurturing hope after loss is like tending a garden after winter's frost. It requires patience, care, and the belief that warmth will return and, with it, the bloom of new life. This is where we start pulling in some of the lessons learned and see how they help foster the power of hope:

- **Gratitude Practice**: Begin each day by naming one thing you're thankful for, aloud or in writing. This simple act can shift focus from what's been lost to the abundance that remains.
- **Visualize Healing**: Spend a few moments daily visualizing yourself gracefully moving through your grief. Imagine the future as a place of peace, where memories bring more joy than pain.
- **Connect with Nature**: Regularly go outside and immerse yourself in natural surroundings. Nature's growth, decay, and rebirth cycle looks like our grieving and healing processes—renewal is a constant part of life.

Future Visions

It is powerful to imagine a future where grief has found its proper place in our story. It means accepting that life can be good again, even if turned upside-down and changed forever. It's not easy when you first start looking toward a future. To foster these visions of the future, consider the following:

- **Letter to Future Self**: Write a letter to yourself, this time from *your* perspective, one year from now. Describe the healing you hope to achieve, the challenges you've overcome, and how you've grown. This can be a powerful way to articulate hopes and expectations for your healing journey.
- **Create a Vision Board**: Compile images, quotes, and items that represent the future you wish to manifest. This visual representation of your hopes and dreams can be a daily reminder of what you're moving toward.

Hope as a Guiding Light

Hope is a guiding light that illuminates your path through the darkness of grief. Hope reminds us that pain and loss are not the end of our story but chapters that contribute to our growth and understanding. Embracing hope as this guiding force involves:

- **Seeking Stories of Hope**: Surround yourself with stories of those who've navigated similar paths of loss and emerged with a renewed sense of purpose. Let their stories inspire and guide you.
- **Affirmations of Hope**: Create personal affirmations that reinforce your belief in the future. Phrases like "I am

moving toward peace and healing each day" can be powerful motivators.

Small Steps Toward Hope

Reclaiming hope and embracing the future is a path we must take one step at a time. No matter how small, these steps are victories, and they deserve to be recognized and celebrated (you remember that, right?). While on this journey toward hope, try a few of these:

- **Set Daily Intentions**: Start each day by setting a simple intention that aligns with hope, such as finding one moment of beauty or acting kindly for someone else.
- **Celebrate the Wins**: Acknowledge every positive step, no matter how minor it seems. Did you manage to enjoy a moment with friends? Did you find yourself smiling at a memory rather than crying? These are signs of hope taking root.
- **Connect with Others**: Hope grows in the company of others. Reach out to friends, join support groups, or engage in community activities. Sharing your journey can multiply hope for you and those around you.

When we start feeling as if we can start looking forward, we begin seeing a horizon teeming with possibility and progress. By nurturing and fostering this hope, we uncover the truth that grief not only destroys us but creates an environment that can lead to profound change, like a new forest growing from the ashes of an old one. Hope reveals that after significant loss, paths to happiness, meaning, and affection remain open, but transformed.

Reflecting on Your PURPOSE Journal

When you're working on your PURPOSE Journal, remember your prompts for **Embrace Personal Growth**: In what ways did you notice yourself growing or changing today, even in the smallest sense? This can be related to resilience, understanding, compassion, or any other area.

Reflect upon what you've learned in this chapter and your feelings. Grab a pen and your journal or a piece of paper, and find a comfortable, serene spot where you can be uninterrupted. Take a moment to breathe deeply, centering yourself, and preparing your heart and mind for this journey inward. We're going to spend some time just focusing on embracing your growth—without feeling guilty about it, and looking at how you face the future. Some of these will resonate now, others not. Come back as needed.

Reflecting on the Echoes of Loss

- Write about the person you were before your loss. What were your defining characteristics, hopes, and fears?
- Now, consider how you've changed since. What aspects of your personality have shifted? Which of your priorities have realigned?
- Think about the silence left after your loved one's departure. How does that silence speak to you, and what does it inspire within you?

The Landscape of Your Heart
You should always be checking in with your emotions:

- Describe your emotional landscape as it currently appears. What emotions are in the foreground? Which are lurking in the shadows?
- Choose an emotion that's been particularly challenging for you. Write a letter expressing everything you feel toward it—anger, fear, acceptance.
- Recall a moment of unexpected joy or peace you've experienced recently. What brought it about? How can you cultivate more moments like it?

Dreams Redirected
- Reflect on a dream or goal you had that's been impacted by your loss. How has your relationship with this dream changed?
- Imagine a conversation with your future self five years from now. What would you want to tell them about the dreams you're pursuing now?
- Think about a passion or interest that's been lying dormant within you. What steps can you take to explore or reignite this passion?

The Wisdom Within
- Write about a lesson loss has taught you, one that you couldn't have learned any other way. How has this lesson shaped your outlook on life?
- Consider the concept of resilience. How have you seen it manifest in your own life? In what ways do you still wish to grow stronger?

- Loss often brings hidden aspects of ourselves into the light. What have you discovered about yourself that surprised you?

Building Bridges to Tomorrow

- Imagine the life you wish to lead, one that honors your past but is firmly rooted in the present. What does it look like? Feel like?
- Describe one small but significant change you can make today that aligns with this vision. How will you implement it?
- Loss reshapes our relationship with time. How has your perception of time changed, and how do you wish to spend the time you have?

Nurturing Your Spirit

- Self-care is vital as you navigate through grief. What does self-care mean to you now, and how has its importance shifted?
- Identify a self-care practice you've neglected but wish to reintroduce into your life. What has been holding you back?
- Gratitude can be a powerful tool for healing. List five things, big or small, that you're grateful for at this moment.

The Art of Letting Go

- Holding on to grief can sometimes feel like holding on to the person we've lost. Write about what letting go means to you. Is it scary? Liberating? Both?

- Think of something related to your loss that you're ready to release—anger, guilt, a particular memory. How do you plan to let it go?
- Letting go doesn't mean forgetting. How do you balance the act of moving forward with the desire to keep your loved one's memory alive?

Crafting Your Narrative

- Every person's grief is a unique story. How would you title the chapter of your life that deals with loss? Why?
- Stories have power—the power to wound but also to heal. Write about a moment in your grief journey that felt like a turning point.
- Consider the narrative you wish to build from here on. What themes do you want it to encompass? Hope? Discovery? Renewal?

Through these prompts, I hope you explore the depths of your experience, confront the past honestly, and recognize where you've shined. As my acting coach has said many times, "Scratch deeper." By doing so, you'll uncover the resilience, wisdom, and hope that loss somehow manages to nurture within us. It also helps us realize that we can actually survive this, and we can actually live a life with happiness.

Motivational Mantras to Thrive, One Day at a Time

E very day presents a new canvas, sometimes smeared with the hues of grief, other times washed in the light of healing. Words have the power to hurt us, or if we focus on our mindset, they have the power to anchor, lift, and propel us forward though our emotions. Mantras, simple yet profound affirmations, serve as these anchors, reminders of our inner strength and resilience despite the waves of sorrow.

The Art of Using Mantras

Before diving into the mantras themselves, let's understand how to integrate them into our daily rhythm effectively:

- **Choose Your Mantra**: Select a mantra that resonates with you deeply. It should be a phrase that speaks to your heart, offering comfort or motivation. Mine is based on the lyrics of a song written by a friend.
- **Morning Ritual**: Incorporate your mantra into your morning routine. Repeat it to yourself while still in bed, making it the first thought that guides your day.
- **Visual Reminders**: Place your mantra in visible spots— on your mirror, the fridge, or as a phone wallpaper. Let its presence be a constant throughout your day. You don't need to go as far as I did to tattoo it on your arm.
- **Breathe and Repeat**: Whenever you feel overwhelmed, take a deep breath and silently repeat your mantra. Let its words wrap around you like a comforting blanket, steadying your heart and mind.

With these practices, mantras become more than mere words; they transform into lifelines, pulling us back to the shore when the sea of grief seems too vast.

Mantras to Illuminate the Path

Some mantras can serve as lighthouse beacons on our journey through grief and healing, reminding us where the ground is safe. Each one brings resilience to our daily experiences. Find one that resonates with you:

- Today, I choose to find beauty in the small things.
- I am a vessel of strength and healing.
- With each breath, I create space for peace and renewal.
- I honor my journey, knowing each step moves me toward light.
- My heart is open to moments of joy amidst the sorrow.
- I allow myself to move with the rhythm of my feelings, knowing none are permanent.
- I embrace my vulnerability as a source of strength.
- In the quiet, I find my strength; in the storm, I find my courage.
- I am surrounded by love, both seen and unseen.
- With grace, I release what I cannot change and welcome the growth that comes from pain.
- I am anchored in hope, guided by the light of those I carry in my heart.
- I grant myself permission to laugh, to cry, to heal in my own time.
- Today, I choose to step forward, carrying my memories as wings, not weights.
- I am a beacon of resilience, shining even on the darkest days.

- My spirit is buoyed by the love I've given and received, a testament to my journey.
- I weave my grief into strength, my tears into pearls of wisdom.

Let these mantras whisper courage into the corners of your mind when the shadows of loss loom large.

As we wrap up this exploration of motivational mantras, remember that each day is a step toward healing. Some days, the road may seem impossible to traverse, shrouded in fog and uncertainty. On others, the sun breaks through, clearly showing our way with moments of peace and clarity. Through it all, these mantras act like a rumble strip on the highway — reminding you to stay in the lane where it's safe. They encourage us to keep moving, one day, one breath, one heartbeat at a time, toward a horizon where hope and renewal await.

Now that you're looking out to the horizon and the potential the future holds, I'd like you to carry your mantra and these words of affirmation forward in your heart. I want you to recognize them as testaments to your strength and spirit. Onward we go—toward new chapters and beginnings, made stronger by the lessons of the past and inspired by the promise of tomorrow. You deserve a good life.

Lighting a Path in the Darkness

Y ou're making your way through an important journey, and along the way, you've gathered a wealth of knowledge to help you renew, define, and fire up your sense of purpose and navigate through grief. Now, it's your turn to light the path for others who are seeking the same guidance and support.

Your experience and insights are invaluable, and by sharing your honest opinion of this book on Amazon, you become a guiding light for others in their moments of darkness. Your review has the power to point fellow seekers in the right direction, showing them where they can find the resources to aid their healing process.

I thank you sincerely for your willingness to help. The journey to recovery from grief is enriched and perpetuated by the wisdom we share. By leaving a review, you're not just contributing to a conversation—you're helping to spread a message of hope and renewal.

Please leave your review on Amazon.

By sharing your thoughts, you're doing more than just recommending a book; you're actively participating in a healing community, offering a beacon of hope to those still finding their way.

Thank you for being an essential part of this journey.

Conclusion

Hey, you. Yes, you, holding this book and walking this incredibly tough path. We've journeyed together through these pages, through the highs and lows of grief, and now we're at this part we call the "conclusion." But know this: your journey, your real, lived-in-the-flesh journey, is still unfolding, and there's only one way it concludes in this life. And that's beautiful.

We've navigated the PURPOSE framework together, right? From Perceiving Reality—acknowledging the raw truth of our loss, through Unburdening ourselves of the heaviness that grief brings, Reaching out for that essential human connection, Probing for what this all means on a personal level, Opening ourselves to the beginnings that follow endings, Saving those precious memories that keep us connected to what we've lost, to

Embracing the growth that often comes from our deepest pain. Each step is a chapter in your unique story of healing.

We've discovered that grief isn't just a shadowy valley to rush through. It's rugged terrain and stormy seas where, surprisingly, new strength is forged, and unexpected paths to personal transformation are revealed. By embracing our grief, we've learned it's possible to find new meanings and purposes that enrich our lives beyond what we might have imagined.

Remember this: your grief journey is uniquely yours. There's no prescribed route or timeline. What you feel and how you heal are yours to own, and they're worthy of every bit of compassion and respect you can muster—not just from others but from yourself, too.

We've armed ourselves with coping strategies. Emotional wellness tools and support mechanisms are all in your toolkit now, ready to be pulled out whenever you need them. These aren't one-and-done solutions; they're companions for your journey, ready to offer support time and time again.

And, oh, the importance of treating yourself with kindness! Healing isn't linear. It zigs and zags, loops back upon itself, and takes off in unexpected directions. Be gentle with yourself through all of it. The transformations in identity that come with grief? They're not just challenges to overcome but opportunities to understand ourselves more deeply so we can live lives rich with meaning and purpose.

Don't ever underestimate the power of reaching out, of making your story part of the shared human experience. Whether you're seeking support or offering it, there's incredible strength in community and in knowing and being reminded that you're not alone.

So, here's my call to action for you: take everything we've explored together and start sketching out your own grief journey plan. Lean into the chapters that touched you most deeply. They're your starting points, your signposts. When you feel other sections start to resonate with you, return to them as you sketch out your life.

And as we part ways (at least, through these pages), I want to leave you with a message of hope and resilience. Yes, grief changes us, but within it are seeds of new beginnings, fresh joys, and profound connections. Your story isn't defined by loss but enriched by the love you carry forward, by the growth you nurture from pain.

Share your story, won't you? In doing so, you create ripples of understanding and empathy for many others that stretch far beyond what you might see.

Lastly, I truly want to thank you. Thank you for entrusting me to walk a part of this journey with you and for your courage in facing one of life's harshest truths.

Here's to you — to your continued journey of healing, discovery, and, yes, even joy. You've got this. And remember, in the grand tapestry of life, every thread, including those frayed by grief, contributes to the strength and beauty of the whole.

Take care, my friend. May your path forward be lit with moments of peace, understanding, and an ever-deepening love for the life you're living, with all its shadows and its light. And, finally, may the memory of your loved one be a blessing.

With gratitude and respect,
James LaVeck

P.S. I invite you to join me on social media (@lifeafterlosses) and subscribe to www.lifeafterlosses.com.

Scan above to leave a review

References

Disclaimer: The following resources were accurate and accessible at the time of writing (early 2024) through the provided links. However, the author cannot ensure their continued availability. Users are encouraged to search for the resources by title and author if the links become unavailable.

- *American Society of Clinical Oncology. (n.d.). Understanding grief within a cultural context. Cancer.Net.* https://www.cancer.net/coping-with-cancer/managing-emotions/grief-and-loss/understanding-grief-within-cultural-context
- *Villines, Z. (2021, April 19). Understanding the physical symptoms of grief. Healthline.* https://www.healthline.com/health/grief-physical-symptoms
- *Bethesda Health Group. (2017, July 21). The benefits of healing with grief support groups. Bethesda Health.* https://bethesdahealth.org/blog/2017/07/21/healing-grief-benefits-support-groups/
- *Smith, M., & Segal, J. (2020, November). Helping someone who's grieving. HelpGuide.org.* https://www.helpguide.org/articles/grief/helping-someone-who-is-grieving.htm
- *Flourish Mindfully. (n.d.). Understanding the evolving stages of grief and healing. Flourish Mindfully.* https://www.flourishmindfully.com.au/blog/evolving-stages-of-grief-and-modern-grief-therapy#:~:text=Modern%20Models%20of%20Grief,different%20from%20person%20to%20person.
- *Thompson, S. (2022, December). Suppressing emotions can harm you—Here's what to do. Psychology Today.* https://www.psychologytoday.com/us/blog/the-truth-about-exercise-addiction/202212/suppressing-emotions-can-harm-you-heres-what-to-do
- *The Conversation. (2021, November 2). Death and dying: how different cultures deal with grief and mourning. The Conversation.* https://theconversation.com/death-and-dying-how-different-cultures-deal-with-grief-and-mourning-197299
- *American Psychological Association. (n.d.). Grief.* https://www.apa.org/topics/grief
- *Bethesda Health. (2017, July 21). Healing grief: Benefits of support groups.* https://bethesdahealth.org/blog/2017/07/21/healing-grief-benefits-support-groups/
- *Cancer.Net. (n.d.). Understanding grief within a cultural context.* https://www.cancer.net/coping-with-cancer/managing-emotions/grief-and-loss/understanding-grief-within-cultural-context

- *Center for Loss & Life Transition. (2023, December). Helping dispel 5 common misconceptions about grief.* https://www.centerforloss.com/2023/12/helping-dispel-5-common-misconceptions-grief/
- *Cleveland Clinic. (n.d.). Grief.* https://my.clevelandclinic.org/health/diseases/24787-grief
- *Cruse Bereavement Care. (n.d.). Five stages of grief.* https://www.cruse.org.uk/understanding-grief/effects-of-grief/five-stages-of-grief/
- *Full Circle Grief Center. (2022, July 6). Different types of grievers.* https://fullcirclegc.org/2022/07/06/different-types-of-grievers/
- *Health.com. (n.d.). Grief.* https://www.health.com/grief-7692761
- *Healthline. (n.d.). Grief physical symptoms.* https://www.healthline.com/health/grief-physical-symptoms
- *HelpGuide. (n.d.). Helping someone who is grieving.* https://www.helpguide.org/articles/grief/helping-someone-who-is-grieving.htm
- *Marie Curie. (n.d.). Physical symptoms of grief.* https://www.mariecurie.org.uk/help/support/bereaved-family-friends/dealing-grief/physical-symptoms-grief
- *Mayo Clinic. (n.d.). Complicated grief.* https://www.mayoclinic.org/diseases-conditions/complicated-grief/symptoms-causes/syc-20360374
- *Mayo Clinic. (n.d.). What is grief?* https://www.mayoclinic.org/patient-visitor-guide/support-groups/what-is-grief
- *Medical News Today. (n.d.). Depression vs. grief.* https://www.medicalnewstoday.com/articles/depression-vs-grief#differences
- *Mind. (n.d.). Experiences of grief.* https://www.mind.org.uk/information-support/guides-to-support-and-services/bereavement/experiences-of-grief/
- *Missing Pieces. (n.d.). Intuitive grief and instrumental grief.* https://www.missingpiecesgrief.org/blog/intuitive-grief-and-instrumental-grief
- *PACES Connection. (n.d.). Debunking the Kubler-Ross five stages of grief.* https://www.pacesconnection.com/blog/debunking-the-kubler-ross-five-stages-of-grief
- *Psych Central. (n.d.). Myths about grief.* https://psychcentral.com/health/myths-about-grief#myths
- *Psychology Today. (2017, July). Why the five stages of grief are wrong.* https://www.psychologytoday.com/us/blog/supersurvivors/201707/why-the-five-stages-grief-are-wrong
- *Psycom. (n.d.). Stages of grief.* https://www.psycom.net/stages-of-grief
- *Strong Winds. (n.d.). Styles of grieving: Blended and dissonant.* https://www.strongwinds.ca/blog/styles-of-grieving-blended-and-dissonant

- *The Recovery Village. (n.d.). Grief myths.*
  https://www.therecoveryvillage.com/mental-health/grief/grief-myths/
- *Verywell Mind. (n.d.). Grief and depression.*
  https://www.verywellmind.com/grief-and-depression-1067237
- *Verywell Mind. (n.d.). Types of grief people may experience.*
  https://www.verywellmind.com/types-of-grief-people-may-experience-7504728
- *Flourish Mindfully. (n.d.). Evolving stages of grief and modern grief therapy.*
  https://www.flourishmindfully.com.au/blog/evolving-stages-of-grief-and-modern-grief-therapy#:~:text=Modern%20Models%20of%20Grief,different%20from%20person%20to%20person.
- *Levinson, J. (2022, December). Suppressing emotions can harm you: Here's what to do. Psychology Today.* https://www.psychologytoday.com/us/blog/the-truth-about-exercise-addiction/202212/suppressing-emotions-can-harm-you-heres-what-to-do
- *The Conversation. (n.d.). Death and dying: How different cultures deal with grief and mourning.* https://theconversation.com/death-and-dying-how-different-cultures-deal-with-grief-and-mourning-197299
- *What's Your Grief. (n.d.). Grief concept care: Continuing bonds.*
  https://whatsyourgrief.com/grief-concept-care-continuing-bonds/
- *Psychology Today. (2022, November). Accepting death is harder than ever.*
  https://www.psychologytoday.com/us/blog/am-i-right/202211/accepting-death-is-harder-than-ever
- *Lifehack. (n.d.). Is it really possible to accept the death of a loved one?*
  https://www.lifehack.org/586480/really-possible-accept-death-loved-one
- *Verywell Mind. (n.d.). Denial as a defense mechanism.*
  https://www.verywellmind.com/denial-as-a-defense-mechanism-5114461#:~:text=Denial%20is%20a%20type%20of,the%20consequences%20of%20that%20reality.
- *RRTampa. (n.d.). Denial as coping mechanism.* https://rrtampa.com/denial-as-coping-mechanism/
- *Verywell Mind. (n.d.). The denial stage of grief: Characteristics and coping.*
  https://www.verywellmind.com/the-denial-stage-of-grief-characteristics-and-coping-5272456#toc-characteristics-of-the-denial-stage-of-grief
- *Choosing Therapy. (n.d.). Denial stage of grief.*
  https://www.choosingtherapy.com/denial-stage-of-grief/
- *PsychAlive. (n.d.). Denial: The danger in rejecting reality.*
  https://www.psychalive.org/denial-the-danger-in-rejecting-reality/
- *Krause Funeral Home. (n.d.). What does denial look like after a loss?*
  https://www.krausefuneralhome.com/blog/what-does-denial-look-like-after-a-loss/

- *Talkspace. (n.d.). How dangerous is denial?*
  https://www.talkspace.com/blog/how-dangerous-is-denial/
- *WebMD. (n.d.). How denial affects your life.* https://www.webmd.com/mental-health/features/how-denial-affects-your-life
- *Lifehacker. (n.d.). How denial negatively affects your choices and what you can do about it.* https://lifehacker.com/how-denial-negatively-affects-your-choices-and-what-yo-5972649
- *Coping.com. (n.d.). Denial.* https://coping.com/denial/
- *Human Infusion Project. (n.d.). 9 misunderstandings about acceptance.* https://www.humaninfusionproject.com/post/9-misunderstandings-about-acceptance
- *Grief Healing Blog. (2013, June). Tips for coping with disbelief and denial in grief.* https://www.griefhealingblog.com/2013/06/tips-for-coping-with-disbelief-and.html
- *Remembering a Life. (n.d.). From death denial to death acceptance.* https://www.rememberingalife.com/blogs/blog/from-death-denial-to-death-acceptance
- *Order of the Good Death. (n.d.). Death positive movement.* https://www.orderofthegooddeath.com/death-positive-movement
- *End With Care. (n.d.). Full Post.* https://www.endwithcare.org/blogs/FullPost.php?id=59
- *Get Urns. (n.d.). How to be positive about death.* https://www.geturns.com/blogs/news/how-to-be-positive-about-death
- *Hospice UK. (n.d.). About death and dying.* https://www.hospiceuk.org/information-and-support/death-and-dying-what-expect/about-death-and-dying
- *St. Clare Hospice. (2020, April). How to talk about death and dying - Guide Ver 2.* https://stclarehospice.org.uk/wp-content/uploads/2020/04/How-to-talk-about-death-and-dying-Guide-Ver-2.pdf
- *Hospice of the Red River Valley. (n.d.). 5 conversation starters to talk about death, dying, end-of-life preferences.* https://www.hrrv.org/blog/5-conversation-starters-to-talk-about-death-dying-end-of-life-preferences
- *Christie Lynn Blog. (2018, April 23). The ugly side of grief that nobody tells you about.* https://www.christielynnblog.com/2018-4-23-the-ugly-side-of-grief-that-nobody-tells-you-about/
- *Santucci, P. (n.d.). The ugly side of grief.* https://www.petesantucci.com/the-ugly-side-of-grief/
- *Hope for Widows Foundation. (2018, October). Grief: It's ugly.* https://hopeforwidows.org/2018/10/grief-its-ugly/
- *Charnas, D. (2016, November). 3 Reasons to let yourself feel your emotions. Psychology Today.* https://www.psychologytoday.com/us/blog/mindful-musings/201611/3-reasons-let-yourself-feel-your-emotions

- *Sage Hill Counseling. (n.d.). The benefits of being able to hurt.* https://www.sagehill.co/blog/the-benefits-of-being-able-to-hurt
- *Scientific American. (n.d.). Negative emotions are key to well-being.* https://www.scientificamerican.com/article/negative-emotions-key-well-being/
- *Greater Good Magazine. (n.d.). Four ways we avoid our feelings and what to do instead.* https://greatergood.berkeley.edu/article/item/four_ways_we_avoid_our_feelings_and_what_to_do_instead
- *Praxis Continuing Education and Training. (n.d.). How avoiding emotions keeps them high intensity.* https://www.praxiscet.com/posts/how-avoiding-emotions-keeps-them-high-intensity/
- *Villines, Z. (2021, September). 8 Ways people avoid their emotions. Psychology Today.* https://www.psychologytoday.com/intl/blog/in-practice/202109/8-ways-people-avoid-their-emotions
- *Conscious Magazine. (n.d.). 5 ways to stop avoiding painful feelings.* https://consciousmagazine.co/5-ways-to-stop-avoiding-painful-feelings/
- *Bono, M. (2022, April). Why sadness is a nonnegotiable part of grief. Psychology Today.* https://www.psychologytoday.com/intl/blog/widows-walk/202204/why-sadness-is-a-nonnegotiable-part-of-grief
- *Center for Loss & Life Transition. (2023, December). Embracing the sadness of grief.* https://www.centerforloss.com/2023/12/embracing-the-sadness-of-grief/
- *Talkspace. (n.d.). How to deal with sadness.* https://www.talkspace.com/blog/how-to-deal-with-sadness/
- *Psych Central. (n.d.). Why you should express your sadness.* https://psychcentral.com/blog/why-you-should-express-your-sadness#_noHeaderPrefixedContent
- *Gundersen Health System. (n.d.). Healthy ways to deal with sadness.* https://www.gundersenhealth.org/health-wellness/live-happy/healthy-ways-to-deal-with-sadness
- *Hospice Foundation of America. (n.d.). Anger and grief.* https://hospicefoundation.org/End-of-Life-Support-and-Resources/Grief-Support/Journeys-with-Grief-Articles/Anger-and-Grief
- *What's Your Grief. (n.d.). Anger in grief makes you angry.* https://whatsyourgrief.com/anger-in-grief-makes-you-angry/
- *Marie Curie. (n.d.). Anger in grief.* https://www.mariecurie.org.uk/talkabout/articles/anger-in-grief/253186
- *Cacciatore, J. (2022, August). 5 power tools to reset grief's anger. Psychology Today.* https://www.psychologytoday.com/us/blog/tales-grief/202208/5-power-tools-reset-griefs-anger

- *Harvard Health Publishing. (n.d.). Coping with anger while grieving.* https://www.health.harvard.edu/mind-and-mood/coping-with-anger-while-grieving
- *Mental Health America. (n.d.). 10 healthy ways to release rage.* https://mhanational.org/10-healthy-ways-release-rage
- *SELF. (n.d.). How to let go of anger.* https://www.self.com/story/how-to-let-go-of-anger
- *Caring Therapists of Broward. (n.d.). Five things you can do today to release anger.* https://caringtherapistsofbroward.com/five-things-you-can-do-today-to-release-anger/
- *Hospice Foundation of America. (n.d.). Guilt: A normal but unnecessary burden.* https://hospicefoundation.org/Grief-(1)/Journeys-with-Grief-Articles/Guilt-A-Normal-but-Unnecessary-Burden
- *Care for the Family. (n.d.). The role of guilt in grief.* https://www.careforthefamily.org.uk/bereavement/the-role-of-guilt-in-grief/
- *My Grief and Loss. (n.d.). Guilt and grief.* https://mygriefandloss.org/guilt-and-grief
- *Happiful. (n.d.). 5 compassionate ways to deal with grief-related guilt.* https://happiful.com/5-compassionate-ways-to-deal-with-grief-related-guilt
- *Psych Central. (n.d.). How to let go of the past and hurt.* https://psychcentral.com/blog/how-to-let-go-of-the-past-and-hurt
- *Mindbodygreen. (n.d.). How to let go of the past.* https://www.mindbodygreen.com/articles/how-to-let-go-of-pas
- *Healthline. (n.d.). How to forgive yourself.* https://www.healthline.com/health/how-to-forgive-yourself#2.-Acknowledge-the-mistake-out-loud
- *Verywell Mind. (n.d.). How to forgive yourself.* https://www.verywellmind.com/how-to-forgive-yourself-4583819
- *My Therapy NYC. (n.d.). Grief and relief.* https://mytherapynyc.com/grief-and-relief/#:~:text=We%20may%20think%20that%20feeling,wanted%20the%20person%20to%20die
- *Marie Curie. (n.d.). Relieved when someone dies.* https://www.mariecurie.org.uk/talkabout/articles/relieved-when-someone-dies/313426
- *Funeral Guide. (n.d.). Coping with feelings of relief during bereavement.* https://www.funeralguide.co.uk/help-resources/bereavement-support/coping-with-bereavement/coping-with-feelings-of-relief-during-bereavement
- *Empathy. (n.d.). Feeling numb after a loss.* https://www.empathy.com/grief/feeling-numb-after-a-loss

- *Psychology Today. (2019, June). Numbed out: When feelings freeze after bereavement.* https://www.psychologytoday.com/us/blog/the-mourning-after/201906/numbed-out-when-feelings-freeze-after-bereavement
- *Sandstone Care. (n.d.). Emotional numbness.* https://www.sandstonecare.com/blog/emotional-numbness/
- *Bradley Funeral Homes. (2018). Volume Three 2018.* https://bradleyfuneralhomes.com/wp-content/uploads/2018/02/VolumeThree_2018web.pdf
- *Join Cake. (n.d.). Why don't I feel anything when someone dies?* https://www.joincake.com/blog/why-dont-i-feel-anything-when-someone-dies/
- *Thriveworks. (n.d.). Grief: Experiencing a flood of emotions & becoming numb.* https://thriveworks.com/help-with/grief-loss/grief-experiencing-flood-emotions-become-numb/
- *Newport Institute. (n.d.). Feeling emotionally numb.* https://www.newportinstitute.com/resources/mental-health/feeling-emotionally-numb/
- *Hospice Foundation of America. (n.d.). Coping with loneliness.* https://hospicefoundation.org/End-of-Life-Support-and-Resources/Grief-Support/Journeys-with-Grief-Articles/Coping-with-Lonliness#:~:text=Loneliness%20is%20a%20natural%20part,separation%20and%20isolation%20from%20others.
- *Cruse Bereavement Care. (n.d.). Grief and loneliness.* https://www.cruse.org.uk/understanding-grief/effects-of-grief/grief-and-loneliness/
- *Beyond Words. (2022, January 25). Understanding the loneliness of grief.* https://www.beyondwordsco.com/blog/2022/1/25/understanding-the-loneliness-of-grief
- *Refuge In Grief. (2021, June 2). Five ways to manage your grief and loneliness.* https://refugeingrief.com/2021/06/02/five-ways-to-manage-your-grief-and-loneliness/
- *British Seniors. (n.d.). Coping with loneliness after losing a loved one.* https://www.britishseniors.co.uk/over-50-life-insurance/coping-with-loneliness-after-losing-a-loved-one/
- *Hospice of the Red River Valley. (n.d.). Loneliness: Grief's unintended guest.* https://www.hrrv.org/blog/loneliness-griefs-unintended-guest/
- *Verywell Mind. (n.d.). How to cope with loneliness.* https://www.verywellmind.com/how-to-cope-with-loneliness-3144939
- *Soulistic Hospice. (n.d.). The importance of seeking connections in times of grief.* https://soulistichospice.org/blog/the-importance-of-seeking-connections-in-times-of-grief

- Saltz, G. (2014, January). *The importance of friends in grief. Psychology Today.* https://www.psychologytoday.com/intl/blog/am-i-right/201401/the-importance-friends-in-grief
- *TAPS. (n.d.). Solitude & social support balance.* https://www.taps.org/articles/25-1/solitude-social-support-balance
- *Mind. (n.d.). Support and self-care.* https://www.mind.org.uk/information-support/guides-to-support-and-services/bereavement/support-and-self-care/
- *Wells San Francisco.* (n.d.). 5 signs that you might need grief counseling. https://wellsanfrancisco.com/5-signs-that-you-might-need-grief-counseling/
- *Calm Sage. (n.d.). Signs you should seek grief counseling.* https://www.calmsage.com/signs-you-should-seek-grief-counseling/
- *Phaneuf. (n.d.). 10 signs that you may need grief counseling.* https://phaneuf.net/blog/10-signs-that-you-may-need-grief-counseling
- *What's Your Grief. (n.d.). Thanks for the offer, but I don't know what I need.* https://whatsyourgrief.com/thanks-for-the-offer-but-i-dont-know-what-i-need/
- *Everplans. (n.d.). How to ask for help after a death.* https://www.everplans.com/articles/how-to-ask-for-help-after-a-death
- *What's Your Grief. (n.d.). Helping friends help you.* https://whatsyourgrief.com/helping-friends-help-you-1/
- *Refuge in Grief. (2022, January 12). Grief: Call me if you need anything.* https://refugeingrief.com/2022/01/12/grief-call-me-if-you-need-anything/
- *Bateman Allen Funeral Home. (n.d.). How to ask for help when grieving.* https://www.batemanallenfuneralhome.com/grief/how-to-ask-for-help-when-grieving/
- *Sturtevant, P. (n.d.). Grief and relationships.* https://paulsturtevant.com/grief-and-relationships/
- *Join Cake. (n.d.). How does grief affect relationships?* https://www.joincake.com/blog/how-does-grief-affect-relationships/#h_927030624741653513900384
- *SD Relationship Place. (n.d.). Grief & relationships: How your relationships might change when facing grief.* https://www.sdrelationshipplace.com/grief-relationships-how-your-relationships-might-change-when-facing-grief/
- *What's Your Grief. (n.d.). How to maintain relationships after a death.* https://whatsyourgrief.com/how-to-maintain-relationships-after-a-death/
- *LinkedIn. (n.d.). How to maintain relationships during bereavement.* https://www.linkedin.com/pulse/how-maintain-relationships-during-bereavement-inscripture?trk=pulse-article
- *Palo Alto Online. (2015, March 10). 7 dos and don'ts for staying connected as a couple during grief.* https://www.paloaltoonline.com/2015/03/10/7-dos-and-donts-for-staying-connected-as-a-couple-during-grief/

- *Calming Tree Counselling. (2018, May 20). Grief: Maintaining relationships.* https://calmingtreecounselling.ca/2018/05/20/grief-maintaining-relationships-kitchener-counselling/
- *CABA. (n.d.). How to talk about feelings.* https://www.caba.org.uk/mental-health/managing-mental-health/how-talk-feelings.html
- *HealthyPlace. (n.d.). How to open up and reveal yourself to others.* https://www.healthyplace.com/relationships/healthy-relationships/how-to-open-up-and-reveal-yourself-to-others
- *Well+Good. (n.d.). How to talk about your feelings.* https://www.wellandgood.com/how-to-talk-about-your-feelings/
- *SMCT. (n.d.). Shared grief can be a comfort.* https://smct.org.au/blog/shared-grief-can-be-a-comfort
- *Hope Mommies. (n.d.). Grieving together: Be honest about your feelings.* https://hopemommies.org/grieving-together-be-honest-about-your-feelings
- *HelpGuide. (n.d.). Helping someone who is grieving.* https://www.helpguide.org/articles/grief/helping-someone-who-is-grieving.htm
- *CancerCare. (n.d.). How to help someone who is grieving.* https://www.cancercare.org/publications/67-how_to_help_someone_who_is_grieving
- *Marie Curie. (n.d.). Supporting a grieving family member or friend.* https://www.mariecurie.org.uk/help/support/bereaved-family-friends/dealing-grief/supporting-a-grieving-family-member-or-friend
- *What's Your Grief. (n.d.). Finding comfort in grief through connection and co-destiny.* https://whatsyourgrief.com/finding-comfort-in-rief-through-connection-and-co-destiny/
- *Clay, J. (n.d.). A new perspective on coping with the death of a loved one. LinkedIn.* https://www.linkedin.com/pulse/new-perspective-coping-death-loved-one-jelani-clay?trk=articles_directory
- *Chopra. (n.d.). Finding purpose in grief and loss.* https://chopra.com/blogs/personal-growth/finding-purpose-in-grief-and-loss
- *Kothari, B. (n.d.). Intentional living: Finding meaning and inner growth from grief. LinkedIn.* https://www.linkedin.com/pulse/intentional-living-finding-meaning-inner-growth-from-grief-kothari-bjkpc
- *Grief Healing. (n.d.). Column: Finding meaning.* https://www.griefhealing.com/column-finding-meaning.htm
- *Hospice of the Red River Valley. (n.d.). 4 tips to deal with happiness guilt.* https://www.hrrv.org/blog/4-tips-to-deal-with-happiness-guilt/
- *Therapy Changes. (2022, August). Learning to be happy again after a loss.* https://therapychanges.com/blog/2022/08/learning-to-be-happy-again-after-a-loss/
- *Option B. (n.d.). Struggle: Grief and joy can coexist.* https://optionb.org/supporting-self/struggle-grief-and-joy-can-coexist

- *Lifehack. (n.d.). 7 reasons why experiencing grief makes you a better person.* https://www.lifehack.org/386632/7-reasons-why-experiencing-grief-makes-you-better-person
- *Possibility Change. (n.d.). How pain, heartache, and loss can make you better.* https://possibilitychange.com/how-pain-heartache-and-loss-can-make-you-better/
- *Grief and Sympathy. (n.d.). The hidden benefits of grief.* https://www.griefandsympathy.com/the-hidden-benefits-of-grief.html
- *Forbes Nonprofit Council. (2021, July 28). Why grief motivates you to become better. Forbes.* https://www.forbes.com/sites/forbesnonprofitcouncil/2021/07/28/why-grief-motivates-you-to-become-better/?sh=73a121db1fdd
- *Eirene Cremations. (n.d.). Using grief to define you.* https://eirenecremations.com/blog/using-grief-to-define-you
- *Thrive Global Community. (n.d.). Don't let your loss define you.* https://community.thriveglobal.com/dont-let-your-loss-define-you/#:~:text=Loss%20should%20not%20define%20who,with%20fondness%20rather%20than%20sadness.
- *A Grieving Twentysomething. (2019, January 4). Grief does not define my life.* https://agrievingtwentysomething.com/2019/01/04/grief-does-not-define-my-life/
- *Chopra. (n.d.). Finding gratitude through grief.* https://chopra.com/blogs/mind-body-health/finding-gratitude-through-grief
- *HuffPost. (n.d.). How grieving with gratitude saved me.* https://www.huffpost.com/entry/how-grieving-with-gratitude-saved-me_b_9282144
- *Join Cake. (n.d.). Grief and gratitude.* https://www.joincake.com/blog/grief-and-gratitude/
- *Hospice Austin. (n.d.). The power of gratitude in grief.* https://www.hospiceaustin.org/the-power-of-gratitude-in-grief/
- *GoodTherapy. (2018, May). When loss hurts: 6 physical effects of grief.* https://www.goodtherapy.org/blog/when-loss-hurts-6-physical-effects-of-grief-0520187
- *WebMD. (2019, July 11). How grief affects your body and mind.* https://www.webmd.com/special-reports/grief-stages/20190711/how-grief-affects-your-body-and-mind
- *Medical News Today. (n.d.). The physical symptoms of grief and loss.* https://www.medicalnewstoday.com/articles/the-physical-symptoms-of-grief-and-loss#how-long-it-lasts
- *Thriveworks. (n.d.). Physical symptoms of grief.* https://thriveworks.com/help-with/grief-loss/physical-symptoms-of-grief/

- *Beyond Blue. (n.d.). Routines.* https://www.beyondblue.org.au/mental-health/routines
- *National Center for Biotechnology Information. (2020, December 31). [PMC article on grief and health].* https://www.ncbi.nlm.nih.gov/pmc/articles/PMC7775995/
- *Better Health Channel. (n.d.). Exercise and mental health.* https://www.betterhealth.vic.gov.au/health/healthyliving/exercise-and-mental-health
- *Wiltshire Wildlife Trust. (n.d.). Healing nature.* https://www.wiltshirewildlife.org/healing-nature
- *Tiny Buddha. (n.d.). 10 steps to find yourself again after loss.* https://tinybuddha.com/blog/10-steps-to-find-yourself-again-after-loss/
- *What's Your Grief. (n.d.). Reconnecting with life after loss.* https://whatsyourgrief.com/reconnecting-with-life-after-loss/
- *Healthline. (n.d.). Mindfulness strategies to cope with loss.* https://www.healthline.com/health/mind-body/mindfulness-strategies-to-cope-with-loss
- *Spirituality & Health. (n.d.). 10 ways to practice mindful grieving.* https://www.spiritualityhealth.com/10-ways-to-practice-mindful-grieving
- *Stang, H. (n.d.). Breathing exercise for grief stress.* https://heatherstang.com/breathing-exercise-for-grief-stress/
- *GoodTherapy. (2012, May 1). Breathing lessons.* https://www.goodtherapy.org/blog/breathing-lessons-0501124
- *Mindful. (n.d.). A 10-minute guided meditation for working with grief.* https://www.mindful.org/a-10-minute-guided-meditation-for-working-with-grief/
- *YouTube. (n.d.). [Video on guided meditation for grief].* https://www.youtube.com/watch?v=lw8VgqHL8_8
- *Well+Good. (n.d.). Body scan meditation for grief.* https://www.wellandgood.com/body-scan-meditation-grief/#:~:text=Breathe%20deeply%2C%20and%20begin%20to%20do%20your%20scan&text=%22Then%2C%20starting%20at%20the%20crown,few%20minutes%20to%20do%20this
- *The Grief Practice. (n.d.). Practices: Body scan.* https://www.thegriefpractice.com/practices/body-scan/
- *Futurity. (n.d.). Grief and progressive muscle relaxation.* https://www.futurity.org/grief-progressive-muscle-relaxation-2617232/
- *Healthline. (n.d.). Progressive muscle relaxation.* https://www.healthline.com/health/progressive-muscle-relaxation#bottom-line
- *Samaritans. (n.d.). The importance of self-care for loss survivors.* https://samaritanshope.org/community-education-outreach/the-importance-of-self-care-for-loss-survivors/

- LifeCare Centres. (2018, May 20). *The importance of self-care during times of grief & loss.* https://lifecarecentres.ca/the-importance-of-self-care-during-times-of-grief-loss/
- Grief Encounter. (n.d.). *Self-care in bereavement.* https://www.griefencounter.org.uk/grief-guide/self-care-in-bereavement/
- Vikara Village. (n.d.). *6 tips for managing insomnia after loss.* https://www.vikaravillage.org/resources/6-tips-for-managing-insomnia-after-loss
- Stang, H. (n.d.). *Grief sleep.* https://heatherstang.com/grief-sleep/
- Saatva. (n.d.). *Grief and sleep.* https://www.saatva.com/blog/grief-and-sleep/
- Memorials of Distinction. (n.d.). *How can exercise help after losing a loved one.* https://www.memorialsofdistinction.co.uk/useful-guides/how-can-exercise-help-after-losing-a-loved-one
- Bakken-Young. (n.d.). *Exercise helps grief.* https://bakken-young.com/exercise-helps-grief/
- COL. (n.d.). *How to cope with grief fitness.* https://www.col.co.uk/help-advice/how-to-cope-with-grief-fitness
- Livestrong. (n.d.). *Workout motivation grief.* https://www.livestrong.com/article/13726330-workout-motivation-grief/
- Psych Central. (n.d.). *Yoga for grief.* https://psychcentral.com/health/yoga-for-grief#grief-yoga-poses
- Learning About Grief. (n.d.). *Yoga poses for grief with pictures.* https://learningaboutgrief.com/blog/yoga-poses-for-grief-with-pictures/
- Yoga With Adriene. (n.d.). *Yoga for grief.* https://yogawithadriene.com/yoga-for-grief/
- Marie Curie. (n.d.). *Nature and grief.* https://www.mariecurie.org.uk/talkabout/articles/nature-and-grief/366915
- Wander Magazine. (n.d.). *Nature for healing grief.* https://wander-mag.com/articles/live-well/nature-for-healing-grief/amp/
- Seeds of Life. (n.d.). *How nature can help your grief journey.* https://www.seedsoflife.com/articles/how-nature-can-help-your-grief-journey
- Funeral Basics. (n.d.). *Nature grief journey.* https://www.funeralbasics.org/nature-grief-journey/
- Edutopia. (n.d.). *7 simple ways to get outside more often.* https://www.edutopia.org/article/7-simple-ways-get-outside-more-often/
- Columbia. (n.d.). *Easy ways to get outside more.* https://www.columbia.com/easy-ways-to-get-outside-more.html
- Total Wellness. (n.d.). *Outdoor time.* https://info.totalwellnesshealth.com/blog/outdoor-time
- Everyday Health. (n.d.). *Start a self-care routine.* https://www.everydayhealth.com/self-care/start-a-self-care-routine/

- *Notes by Thalia. (n.d.). Build a simple self-care routine.* https://notesbythalia.com/build-a-simple-self-care-routine/
- *Marie Curie. (n.d.). Self-care grieving.* https://www.mariecurie.org.uk/talkabout/articles/self-care-grieving/315383
- *Beyond Blue. (n.d.). Routines.* https://www.beyondblue.org.au/mental-health/routines
- *National Center for Biotechnology Information. (2020). [PMC article on mental health].* https://www.ncbi.nlm.nih.gov/pmc/articles/PMC7775995/
- *Better Health Channel. (n.d.). Exercise and mental health.* https://www.betterhealth.vic.gov.au/health/healthyliving/exercise-and-mental-health
- Wiltshire Wildlife Trust. (n.d.). Healing nature. https://www.wiltshirewildlife.org/healing-nature
- *Psychology Today. (2012, July). Death does not end a relationship.* https://www.psychologytoday.com/intl/blog/no-one-has-be-alone/201207/death-does-not-end-relationship
- *Use Your Damn Skills. (2020, February 12). Death doesn't end relationships; it changes them.* https://useyourdamnskills.com/2020/02/12/death-doesnt-end-relationships-it-changes-them/
- *What's Your Grief. (n.d.). Grief is love we only find in loss.* https://whatsyourgrief.com/gief-is-love-we-only-find-in-loss/
- *GoodTherapy. (2018, January 19). Grieve for good: Honor loved one's memory by moving forward.* https://www.goodtherapy.org/blog/grieve-for-good-honor-loved-ones-memory-by-moving-forward-0119185
- *Forbes Nonprofit Council. (2021, October 6). How to honor someone after loss. Forbes.* https://www.forbes.com/sites/forbesnonprofitcouncil/2021/10/06/how-to-honor-someone-after-loss/?sh=c232491a9ff2
- *Insular Life. (n.d.). How to honor a loved one's legacy.* https://www.insularlife.com.ph/articles/how-to-honor-a-loved-one-s-legacy-00000215
- *Experience Camps. (2019, December 4). Four ways to honor someone's memory and keep their legacy alive.* https://experiencecamps.org/blog/2019-12-4-four-ways-to-honor-someones-memory-and-keep-their-legacy-alive
- *Choosing Therapy. (n.d.). Death anniversary.* https://www.choosingtherapy.com/death-anniversary/
- *Hospice of the Red River Valley. (n.d.). Healthy ways to keep memories alive.* https://www.hrrv.org/grief-support/healthy-ways-keep-memories-alive/#:~:text=Your%20ritual%20might%20be%20a,may%20seek%20less%20tangible%20ways
- *Radiant Roots. (n.d.). Staying present in the face of grief and loss.* https://radiant-roots.co.uk/resources/grief/staying-present-in-the-face-of-grief-and-loss/#8-suggestions--staying-present-in-the-face-of-grief-and-loss

- Hibbert, C. (n.d.). *Grief & loss: Dealing with death anniversaries, birthdays & holidays.* https://www.drchristinahibbert.com/grief-loss-dealing-with-death-anniversaries-birthdays-holidays/
- The Psychology Group. (n.d.). *How to cope with grief during the holidays.* https://thepsychologygroup.com/how-to-cope-with-grief-during-the-holidays/
- VITAS Healthcare. (n.d.). *Coping with grief during the holidays.* https://www.vitas.com/family-and-caregiver-support/grief-and-bereavement/holidays-and-grief/coping-with-grief-during-the-holidays
- McSwain, S., Finnegan, B., & Espenshade, D. (n.d.). *How to help handle special days and holidays.* https://msbfh.com/129/How-to-Help-Handle-Special-Days-and-Holidays.html
- Cruse Bereavement Care. (n.d.). *Coping with anniversaries and reminders.* https://www.cruse.org.uk/understanding-grief/managing-grief/coping-with-anniversaries-and-reminders/
- American Institute of Health Care Professionals. (2024, February 29). *Grief journaling for healing.* https://aihcp.net/2024/02/29/grief-journaling-for-healing/
- Volunteering Australia. (n.d.). *Evidence insights: Volunteering and mental health.* https://www.volunteeringaustralia.org/wp-content/uploads/Evidence-Insights-Volunteering-and-mental-health-Final.pdf
- Forsythia, S. (n.d.). *Four tips for goal setting after a loss. Medium.* https://shelbyforsythia.medium.com/four-tips-for-goal-setting-after-a-loss-82737c9123e3
- Aeon. (n.d.). *Why bereavement turns to activism in a grief-averse culture.* https://aeon.co/essays/why-bereavement-turns-to-activism-in-a-grief-averse-culture
- VITAS Healthcare. (n.d.). *What is grief? Suffering loss.* https://www.vitas.com/family-and-caregiver-support/grief-and-bereavement/what-is-grief/suffering-loss
- What's Your Grief. (n.d.). *Don't know who I am anymore: Grief & loss of identity.* https://whatsyourgrief.com/dont-know-anymore-grief-loss-identity/
- Empathy. (n.d.). *When grief makes you lose sight of who you are.* https://www.empathy.com/grief/when-grief-makes-you-lose-sight-of-who-you are
- The Shift. (n.d.). *5 ways to shift mindset & see change as an opportunity.* https://theshift.fi/5-ways-shift-mindset-see-change-opportunity/
- The Saturday Evening Post. (2019, June). *Four steps to making change an opportunity, not a threat.* https://www.saturdayeveningpost.com/2019/06/four-steps-to-making-change-an-opportunity-not-a-threat/
- Lifehack. (n.d.). *Learn to let go.* https://www.lifehack.org/847748/learn-to-let-go

- *Hack Spirit. (n.d.). Ways to learn to let go of what you can't control.* https://hackspirit.com/ways-to-learn-to-let-go-of-what-you-cant-control/
- *BetterHelp. (n.d.). How to stop caring about things you can't control.* https://www.betterhelp.com/advice/stress/how-to-stop-caring-about-things-you-cant-control/
- *Psychology Today. (2015, November). 10 things you can do to create a new life after any loss.* https://www.psychologytoday.com/us/blog/widows-guide-healing/201511/10-things-you-can-do-create-new-life-after-any-loss
- *Life's Never Dull. (n.d.). How to reinvent yourself.* https://www.lifesneverdull.com/how-to-reinvent-yourself/
- *Lucidchart Blog. (n.d.). 7 steps to creating better goals.* https://www.lucidchart.com/blog/7-steps-to-creating-better-goals
- *BetterUp. (n.d.). How to set goals and achieve them.* https://www.betterup.com/blog/how-to-set-goals-and-achieve-them
- *BetterUp. (n.d.). Comfort zone.* https://www.betterup.com/blog/comfort-zone
- *Indeed Career Guide. (n.d.). Getting out of your comfort zone.* https://www.indeed.com/career-advice/career-development/getting-out-of-your-comfort-zone
- *Indeed Career Guide. (n.d.). Discover core values.* https://www.indeed.com/career-advice/career-development/discover-core-values#:~:text=To%20learn%20about%20your%20values,are%20important%20values%20for%20you.
- *Forbes Coaches Council. (2022, February 18). 15 effective ways to discover and articulate your core values. Forbes.* https://www.forbes.com/sites/forbescoachescouncil/2022/02/18/15-effective-ways-to-discover-and-articulate-your-core-values/?sh=35467bc1df1f
- *Psych Central. (n.d.). Discover your values.* https://psychcentral.com/blog/discover-your-values#tips-to-find-your-values
- *Psych Central. (n.d.). How to find sense of purpose when depressed.* https://psychcentral.com/depression/how-to-find-sense-of-purpose-when-depressed#finding-purpose-again
- *Grief In Common. (n.d.). Finding purpose in loss.* https://www.griefincommon.com/blog/finding-purpose-loss/
- *Experience Camps. (2020, April 15). PraHow to find purpose after someone we love dies.* https://experiencecamps.org/blog/2020-4-15-how-to-find-purpose-after-someone-we-love-dies
- *University of Edinburgh. (n.d.). Values.* https://www.ed.ac.uk/reflection/reflectors-toolkit/self-awareness/values
- *Speak of Money. (n.d.). 16 questions to discover your core values and purpose.* https://www.speakofmoney.com/financial-planning-basics/16-questions-to-discover-your-core-values-and-purpose/
- *Grief Recovery Houston. (n.d.). Managing bad depression days.* https://www.griefrecoveryhouston.com/managing-bad-depression-days/

- *The Grief Toolbox. (n.d.). 20 ways to get through those bad days.*
  https://thegrieftoolbox.com/article/20-ways-get-through-those-bad-days
- *Plentiful Life Counselling. (n.d.). Grief: How to cope with the bad days.*
  https://plentifullifecounselling.com.au/wp/grief-how-to-cope-with-the-bad-days/

Printed in Great Britain
by Amazon

49343079R00109